The Architecture of the Hindus

THE ARCHITECTURE OF THE HINDUS

— Edited and Revised Edition —

Ram Raz

Introduction by
B.M. Pande

Aryan Books International
New Delhi

THE ARCHITECTURE OF THE HINDUS

ISBN: 978-81-7305-549-2

First Published: 1834

Reprinted after fresh typesetting, editing, additions and new introduction
in **2016** by:

Aryan Books International
Pooja Apartments, 4B, Ansari Road, New Delhi-110 002 (India)
Tel.: 23287589, 23255799; Fax: 91-11-23270385
E-mail: aryanbooks@gmail.com

Designed and Printed in India by
ABI Prints & Publishing Co., New Delhi

Introduction

Ram Raz's essay on Hindu architecture is a pioneering work based on the study of Hindu temple architecture as described in ancient texts on the subject. After unremitting search, Ram Raz succeeded in having in his "possession four standard treatises on architecture" among which *Mānasara* was one. Pursuing his inquiry into the subject, he was able to trace from the "memorial verses preserved among the artists," the titles of sixty-four treatises on architecture. Of these sixty-four, he was able to discern thirty-two *mukhya* or principal and thirty-two *upa* or subordinate treatises on architecture and sculpture. He also consulted Cammata (Kammata) sculptor "who is well-acquainted with the practical part of the Hindu architecture, and with most of the terms used in the art". Interestingly, while lauding William Jones' contribution to and knowledge of Indian literature, he disagreed with his views about the lack of existence of treatises dealing with sacred architecture and sculpture.

Ram Raz very clearly defined what is meant by *Śilpa-śāstra* which is pre-eminently applied to architecture. In his penchant for information, he also took into account the 15th century Tamil work *Iru-samaya-villakam* which though is about refutation of Śaiva doctrines by a Vaishṇava, refers to certain passages from the *Śilpa-śāstra.* As pointed out by Ram Raz, this work "recognizes a great number of treatises (on *Śilpa-śāstra*) and enumerates twenty-nine of them by their titles, concluding the list with the words 'and others'." Among these, Ram Raz mentions *Mānasara, Mayamata, Kaśyapa, Vaikhānasa, Sakaladhikāra, Viśvakarmīya, Sanatkumāra, Sārasvatyam, Pañcharātram;* of these texts are found "scattered remains" in southern India. That Ram Raz was able to trace and collect mutilated fragments of these treatises clearly suggest his single-minded pursuit of the subject.

Ram Raz mainly based his work on *Mānasara,* the contents of which he enunciates in detail. Each *adhyāya* or chapter, 58 in number, provides instruction on practically all aspects of architecture, from selection of the ground to the form of the temple and its various components. Ram Raz could acquire the text only partially which contained 41 instead of 58 chapters.

Mayamata is the other work that Ram Raz was able to acquire. He compared the contents of this work with that of *Mānasara.* Very appropriately, Ram Raz points out the reference about Maya as mentioned in the *Rāmāyaṇa* and the *Mahābhārata* and ascribes to him the authorship of *Sūryasiddhānta*, the reputed work on astronomy.

The main contents and features of the other works are also briefly described and how they differ from each other. Ram Raz's attempt to assess the age of these texts and their provenance ascribing their having been composed in south India is quite convincing.

Two points need to be mentioned here which show his close observation. To put in Ram Raz's words: "The most interesting circumstance connected with these treatises is their toleration of the worship of the Jainas and Bauddhas .... and having likewise prescribed rules for constructing images of the objects of adoration by these sects." The other point is about the probable date of texts. According to Ram Raz, "they prove by internal evidence that they were written at a period subsequent to the canonization of the Apper, Sundarer, Sammander, Manicyavasarer .... several of whom are supposed to have lived between the third and fifth century....". At the same time, he also mentions that the passages referring to these sages are "modern interpolations".

The essay concludes with brief but important account about the mode of preparing *chunam* which is an essential ingredient in both architecture and sculpture, particularly stucco work.

Posthumously published, Ram Raz's formidable work on Hindu architecture could be ranked as a classic. His comparison of Hindu architecture with the Greek, Egyptian or later European architecture shows his depth of understanding without being dogmatic.

The clear and detailed description of the temple and its different components is marked by lucidity. From the qualities of an architect (*śilpi lakshaṇam*) to the several measurements used in architecture, sculpture, etc., selection of the ground and connected matters, Ram Raz has hardly left any aspect on the subject.

Forty-eight plates illustrate the different parts of the temple such as the *upapīṭhas* or pedestals with name given to each portion, *adhisṭhāna* or base, *stambha* or pillars with details about their dimensions, forms, ornaments and capital, different categories of *vimāna* ranging from a single storey to fifteen storeys, *gopuras* and their entrance gateway, etc. Ram Raz also brings out the difference between the Indian orders *vis-à-vis* the Grecian and Roman orders as well as the Egyptian ones.

These illustrations in themselves provide useful information and have added to the usefulness of the work. Ram Raz's diligence and assiduousness is not only reflected in this work but also in his career. Born under indigent circumstances, he learnt English and started as a clerk and thereafter became *Vakil* to the regiment. Recognizing his qualities, he was appointed Head of the College of Fort St. George and subsequently Head English Master. Finally, he rose to the position of Judge and Magistrate. A versatile person, Ram Raz was well-versed in different subjects and branches of learning which is reflected in the present work.

New Delhi
1st October, 2015

B.M. Pande
Director (Retd.)
Archaeological Survey of India

Publisher's Note

The spiritual aspects of Hindu culture are commonly known. However, the achievements of ancient Hindus in various fields of arts and sciences are not that well documented. The information on this heritage is embedded in several old texts and treatises.

It has long been known that ancient Hindus possessed treatises on architecture of an early date prescribing the rules of construction. Most of these treatises were in Sanskrit and of little use to the actual practitioners, many of whom came from the lower orders of society and were denied the benefits of the Sanskrit language. The consequence has been, as Ram Raz so succinctly points out, ''that while the practical part of the science continued to be followed up amongst them as a kind of inheritance, the theory became gradually lost''. Thus, in spite of some of the grand and magnificent temples and sculptures, very few texts are known today describing the principles behind their construction.

Besides, much study needs to be done regarding the practical aspects of these texts. Adam Hardy, while introducing his latest work, *Theory and Practice of Temple Architecture in Medieval India*, poses several questions regarding these texts and their relationship to practice, "…. Who wrote them, priests or practitioners? Who used them, connoisseurs or craftsmen? Do they seek to control practice, or to confer authority? Do they describe practice, or guide it, or inspire it? Do they aim to reveal, or partly to conceal? Do they create norms, or mnemonics? Are they an inventory of tradition, or are they inventing it?"

It is thus important to rediscover these texts as also the tradition. However, the efforts by the concerned institutions/departments to bring these treatises to light have been too few and far between. After the pioneering and monumental series by Prasanna Kumar Acharya on the *Manasara* in the 1930s, not much has been achieved.

Ram Raz's essay on Hindu Architecture is one of the first works in English language on the subject. His contribution needs to be recognized. Also sustained efforts should be made to take it forward. The reprinting of this monograph with a new introduction by Shri B.M. Pande and fresh typesetting is one small step in the direction.

Preface

The introduction to the European public of an "Essay on Hindu Architecture," and by a Hindu, would seem to mark an epoch not only in the history of the science but also in that of the Hindus themselves.

Their palaces, their temples, the stupendous pyramidal gateways leading to the latter, the colonnades and porticoes with which they are surrounded; some of "a thousand pillars," others equally remarkable for their elevations, richness, and grandeur of design, have for ages been the objects of admiration to the traveller in the East; and, though it had long been known, proverbially, that the Hindus possessed treatises on architecture of a very ancient date, prescribing the rules by which these edifices were constructed, it remained for the author of this essay to overcome the many, and almost insurmountable, obstacles to the substantiation of the fact, and to the communication of it to the European world in a well-known language of Europe.[1]

As of most other sciences among the Hindus, the rules and precepts of architecture and sculpture had been, with some solitary exceptions, locked up in the Sanskrit language, and, as the study of this language was limited, in general, to the higher classes, the only means of improvement left to the artist, who in all cases would be of a subordinate class, were the verbal instructions delivered to him by these superiors, when they might happen to require his assistance, together with the impress on his mind resulting from practical experience. To reduce the knowledge thus acquired to a system, and to promulgate it in a language comprehensible by the vulgar, would, in most cases, have been thought an encroachment on the privileges of the higher orders; and being, therefore, handed down

1. The Royal Asiatic Society is chiefly indebted to one of its members, Richard Clarke, Esq., for the accomplishment of this important and desirable object. This gentleman, then recently returned from India, suggested to Ram Raz to undertake some work, which should impart to the European world, through the Royal Asiatic Society, information not yet before them; and he recommended the "Architecture of the Hindus" as a topic worthy of the abilities and talents of his native friend. The circumstances under which he acceded to the proposition, though already brought to the notice of the public in "Rickards's India," merit and indeed claim insertion in an introduction to his work. They are detailed in two letters from the author to Mr. Clarke, extracts from which will be found in a subsequent page.

unavoidably from father to son by tradition only, it must, in the natural course of events, have been often obscured or totally lost. Moreover, the study of this, as well as of other sciences, has been very generally laid aside by the higher classes for acquirements more in unison with the tone and feelings of the times; while the treatises themselves, scattered and neglected, became nearly valueless to all but the humble artisan, who gathered up here and there a fragment, and hoarded the occult lore, sometime to be learnt by stealth, or as best might suit the purpose of his lordly and priestly master.

To collect these remains from far and near; to read, collate, and comprehend them, with the terms and phraseology of the science, was no ordinary undertaking: the assistance of the artist on the one hand, of philologists on the other; corroboration by reference to existing edifices, and the ability to exhibit the results at length deduced, in the technical and scientific language of a foreign people, were all equally necessary to the completion of the task.

It must, however, be understood that the author does not profess to give the whole system of architecture as known to the Hindus at any particular period, or indeed, a complete translation of such portions of those treatises as he was able to collect; but, from his deductions and illustrations, such an exposition as might enable the European reader to form an opinion of what that system may once have been.

Such was the attempt of Ram Raz.[1] How far he has been successful the public must decide. Men,[2] whose authority will, it is believed, be readily acknowledged, have spoken of his· work in terms of the highest commendation; and if it shall appear that he has established the claim of his countrymen to the possession, in an eminent degree, of a knowledge in the art—and this at a period when its principles were but little understood among Europeans, he will have accomplished a task which he fondly looked forward to with every confidence of success; and one, it is hoped, which cannot be uninteresting, or devoid of utility, to the followers and promoters of science in general.

The present may not be an improper occasion, as the author of the accompanying essay is no more, to offer a few brief notices of his life. They are, however, merely such as the recollections of the writer to whom the subject of these notices was intimately known for several years, can supply, yet they may, perhaps, as a tribute to his memory, be received with indulgence.

Ram Raz was born at Tanjore, in the Carnatic, about the year 1790. He was small of stature, of a delicate frame, of a fair complexion for an Asiatic, and had a remarkably brilliant and piercing eye. On public occasions there was in his manner, though on the whole graceful and easy, a diffidence which might lead the cursory observer to undervalue his abilities; but by those to whom he was known in private, it was more justly attributed to innate modesty and humility. His name implies that he was of a superior caste; and he used to boast of being a collateral descendant of Ram Raj, or Ram Raz,[3] the last of the

1. It is painful to state that before the result of his labours has passed through the press, accounts from India have announced the decease of this most worthy member of the Royal Asiatic Society.
2. Messrs. William Wilkins, R.A., William Daniell, R.A., and Charles Cockerell, F.S.A.—(*Vide the Tenth Annual Report of the Royal Asiatic Society*, p. 29.)
3. *Raj* or *Raja*, according to the Sanscrit pronunciation: *Raz* or *Raza*, according to the pronunciation of the same term in the vernacular languages of the South of India.

kings of Vijayanagar; and as the name is often met with in the genealogy of those princes, it is not improbable that it may have thus descended to him.

His parents, it would seem, were poor; and that he was partly indebted to fortuitous circumstances for the little education which he received when a boy; a portion of this, however, fortunately for him, consisted in learning to read and write the English language. He was first attached to one of the Native Regiments of Infantry, as a clerk, it is believed, to the Adjutant; and, subsequently, as *Vakil,* or native agent to the regiment. While in these situations he prosecuted the study of the English language; and by acquiring a more grammatical knowledge of the several[1] vernacular dialects which he had been taught in early life, he added to a character for natural quickness of intellect and correctness of conduct, that of an accomplished interpreter. How long he remained in this situation, or whether leaving it at this period he obtained any other, is not known; but in the year 1815, we find him employed as a clerk in the office of the Military Auditor General. While in this employment, a circumstance accidently brought him to the notice of the gentleman before mentioned. He had undertaken to translate from the Mahratta into the English language a code of Regulations drawn up by order of the late Tipu Sultan, the sovereign of Mysore, for the guidance of his revenue officers. Such a work, it will be readily conceived, could not form a part of his duties as clerk in a military audit office, and it must therefore have been a voluntary task.

His translation was in every respect so correct, and the notes and illustrations accompanying it exhibited so eminent a degree of knowledge in the several languages from which the terms and phrases used in the original were generally borrowed, as well as of the Mahratta and English, and at the same time displayed so much talent in the elucidation of the various parts of the subject by comparison and by contrast with the English system of revenue, as at that period to give rise to considerable doubt of its being the unassisted performance of a Hindu. Satisfied that it was so, this gentleman, his early patron, who besides the several offices which he held in the civil department of the Madras Government, was also Senior Member of the College of Fort St. George, gladly availed himself of so fair an opportunity to countenance and encourage talents and conduct such as he observed in our author; and procured for him, first, the appointment of Head of the College Office, and afterwards that of Head English Master to the native classes of that institution.

It was while in the latter situation that he was, for upwards of five years, intimately known to the writer of these remarks, who, shortly before his quitting India, had the satisfaction of recommending him to the First Commissioner in Mysore, by which means he was placed in a sphere of action where talents such as his could not long remain unknown, and which soon raised him to the responsible and highly honourable post of Judge and Magistrate.

By a regular course of private study while at Madras, he had added to his other accomplishments, not only a knowledge of the Sanskrit language, but also of algebra,

1. It is not uncommon that in the same town or village, two, three, or more vernacular languages will equally prevail; and that boys are taught, though very imperfectly, to read and write in the whole of them.

geometry, the higher branches of mathematics, and of geography and astronomy; and at one time he had classes in these branches of science, the scholars of which were an honour to his industry and talents; by many of whom his assiduity, ability, and zeal will be long held in grateful remembrance.

Of his death no particular accounts have yet been received. It is said that the climate of Mysore was not congenial to him; and perhaps the duties of his situation there were too arduous for his weakly frame. He had no family, but he had adopted a daughter whom, together with his widow, an aged mother, and a brother who was in some mercantile profession at Madras, he has, it is supposed, left to enjoy the little wealth which his frugality, rather than any adequate return actually awarded to his merits, enabled him to realise. But, however this may have been, his loss as a man of talents and of science, as well as a highly valuable servant of the British Government, is deeply to be regretted.

The writer[1] of these remarks has the pleasure to announce that he expects shortly to receive from the friends of the deceased, ample materials whence a full and authentic view of the author's life may be drawn, should such a record be thought sufficiently interesting to the public, to induce its acceptance by the Royal Asiatic Society.

---

1. After the volume was sent to press, he received from the widow of the deceased a letter, from which the following is an extract:

To Captain HARKNESS

"Bangalore, East-Indies, 22nd May 1833.

* * * *

"As my late husband in his lifetime had mentioned to me the existence of a friendship between yourself and him, and which, by letters found after his decease, I feel convinced existed in your mind towards him, I have taken the liberty to address you on the subject of my misfortune, not only in the loss of one so dear, so amiable, but also in being subjected to the mercenary and avaricious views of his brother.

"I beg to call to your remembrance the number of years my late husband was in the Honourable Company's service; first, as Vakeel to the Second Battalion of the Sixteenth Regiment of Madras Native Infantry; then in the Military Auditor General's Office; next in the College at Madras; and, lastly, as Native Judge in the Hoossor Adawlut Court at Bangalore, embracing a period of twenty-three years, during which he never failed in his different situations to obtain the respect and approbation of his superiors, and everyone who had an acquaintance with him, as the various letters and testimonials from highly respectable individuals now in my poseession will testify. It may also be in your recollection that he constantly and steadily pursued a course of study which has tended, in a certain degree, to the embellishment of Oriental Literature. His contributions to the London Asiatic Society, of which he was a corresponding Member, and his Illustrations of the Architecture of Hindostan, and other efforts of his genius, have obtained the public thanks of that Society, and of other learned individuals both here and in England."

Extract of a Letter from RAM RAZ *to* RICHARD CLARKE, *Esq.*
dated Madras, 13th October 1827.

"Since my last letter to you, I have collected ample materials for an essay on our architecture. I am now engaged in examining them, and hope to be able to send you the result of my examination by the next season. Works on *Silpa Sastra* are very scarce in this part of the country; and even the few scattered fragments that can be had are scarcely intelligible to our best educated pundits, as they are so full of memorial verses and technical terms, that none but those who have been regularly initiated in the study of the art, can comprehend them fully. As to our *Silpis* themselves, you know they are generally men of very limited acquirements, and totally unacquainted with the science, so that the task of explaining this obscure subject has become exceedingly difficult. I often attempted to unravel it with the assistance of many artists and pundits who had been supposed to know anything of the matter, and as often despaired of meeting with any success; at length I have fortunately found a good sculptor of the *Cammata* tribe, a native of Tanjore, who is well acquainted with the practical part of the Hindu architecture, and with most of the terms used in the art. With his valuable aid I have already been enabled to solve many intricate problems, and to remove many difficulties against which I had long been struggling. It is a melancholy truth, that those venerable sages to whom our works on arts and sciences are attributed, in endeavouring to communicate instruction to the world, have been guided rather by a mistaken ambition of rendering themselves reputable by the difficulty and abstruseness of their style, than by an anxiety to make themselves intelligible. And to this indeed is that almost general ignorance among the Hindus in the arts and sciences chiefly ascribable. I have now in my possession four standard treatises on architecture, and expect to have some more from different provinces; and I confidently hope that the result of my investigation will enable me to present to the Royal Asiatic Society, through you, a correct account of a science which may be now considered as almost lost for want of encouragement to study it."

To RICHARD CLARKE, *Esq.*

"Madras, 18th January 1828.

"In the last letter which I did myself the honour of addressing to you, I expressed a hope that I should be able to forward to you an Essay on Hindu Architecture by an early opportunity; but I fear I have been too premature in forming such a hope. I little calculated upon the time that would be necessarily required for me to surmount the various difficulties with which I have to contend in elucidating a subject now so little known in this part of the country. Little did I foresee the extent of the field into which my research has since led me. It is true I have procured several treatises on architecture, sculpture, etc.; and I have already mentioned to you how much I am indebted to Dr. Aitkin for the two manuscripts which he had the kindness to procure me; but our best pundits have given them up as altogether inexplicable; and although these works are all composed in Sanskrit, yet, with the exception of some topics connected with religious rites, sacrifices, and astrology (which occupy indeed a considerable portion of the *Silpa Sastra,* and with which we have no immediate concern), I might, without any exaggeration, affirm that the whole is no more intelligible than the darkest oracles are, at least, to those who are unacquainted with the science itself. Our pundits, it is well known, are skilful enough in scholastic disputation respecting grammar, logic, and law; to which, perhaps, may be added, a qualification, though less general, in mythological poetry and metaphysics and a partial knowledge of astronomy and medicine; but our architecture, sculpture, painting, etc. have been for ages confined to a class of people whom our ancient legislators have ranked amongst the lower orders of society. This class, perhaps, jealous of the Brahmans, whose sacerdotal authority they have always opposed with a spirit of independence, or more naturally, apprehensive of competition in their trade, took particular care to conceal the sacred volumes which have descended to them, from the rest of the people; but as they have on their own part been long denied the benefit of Sanskrit literature, these treatises could be but of little use to themselves;

and the consequence has been, that while the practical part of the science continued to be followed up amongst them as a kind of inheritance from generation to generation, the theory became gradually lost to the whole nation, if not to the whole world. Even the few scattered fragments which have escaped the hand which either jealousy or the fear of competition has raised to conceal or rather destroy the science, are now quite unavailable to those who kept them to themselves and to the priests. The former being compelled to refer to the latter for the interpretation of the superior dialect, and the latter to seek from the former for definitions of technical terms, which neither the one nor the other seem to have been able to explain or understand accurately. This circumstance, more than any other, has cost me considerable time and expense, without any adequate advantage. Our best dictionaries, at least the best that I have been able to procure, do not contain a single architectural term, and the best of our workmen have been so long disused to their own ancient style of building durable public edifices, that it is not to be wondered at they should now ascribe their ignorance of the art as revealed from heaven to the want of encouragement, which appears indeed to have ceased on the decline of native rule. Such is the state of knowledge among those to whom we could look for any illustration respecting an art, the study of which has been so long neglected in this country; and the few manuscripts too, which have escaped the corroding hand of time inevitably contain numerous errors and defects, which it requires no small labour and time, to correct and supply.

"These difficulties, combined with want of time on my own part to surmount them, discouraged me for a long while, and it is but lately I commenced to translate and to take down extracts and notes of some parts which I have been enabled to make out. There still remains a great deal to be done; nevertheless, great reason have I to think that what I have already executed will facilitate my future progress. At all events, if it please heaven, I hope to be able to send you at least a part of the work by an early opportunity: and though I cannot promise that my performance will be such as to meet with the approbation of the Royal Asiatic Society, yet I trust it may not prove altogether unacceptable to that learned body of men, inasmuch as it may tend to draw attention to this important subject, connected as it is with the state of arts and sciences in India in early days.

"The subject itself is curious, and highly deserving the attention of the antiquarian and the philosopher. A correct account and accurate elucidation of the art of building practised by the Hindus must throw considerable light on the early progress of architecture in general. Some of the western authors have traced a certain resemblance in the leading features of the buildings in Egypt and India, and have thence concluded that there has very early been a communication of architectural knowledge between the two countries. But it is not altogether improbable that this resemblance may be merely owing to accident; inasmuch as in architecture as well as in every other art indispensably necessary to the comfort of mankind, two or more nations may possess something in common, without having any intercourse with each other, for the wants felt by man being the same, it is not surprising that the remedies resorted to for supplying them should be also similar or nearly so. If, on the other hand, however, both these countries had actually any communication in early ages, it is hard to determine which of them may have been indebted to the other. The western writers on antiquities have not placed this matter beyond a doubt. And for my own part, I will not venture to affirm anything with certainty, until I have collected sufficient information to form an opinion as to this alleged affinity in the architecture of Egypt and India. I humbly presume, therefore, that until the *Silpa Sastra* of the Hindus is correctly illustrated and laid before the public, the question as to whether the art owes its origin to the one or the other of the two countries must remain problematical.

"Whilst the subject of my present research opens upon me such a wide field of delightful prospect notwithstanding the difficulties I already anticipated, I cannot but acknowledge, with painful sensations, my own incompetency for the task which your kindness has assigned to me, and regret most sincerely that it has not fallen into able hands. Diligence and fidelity, however, in the execution of the work entrusted to me shall not be wanting on my part; but the result of my labours can be only commensurate to the ability I possess compared with the difficulty of the subject.

"I hope what I have already said will give you some notion of the nature of the undertaking in which I am engaged, and of the little progress which I have hitherto been enabled to make in consequence of unavoidable delays arising partly from the difficulty of the subject, and partly from the want of leisure. You are too well acquainted with my trifling acquirements to entertain high expectations in the performance of the task assigned to me. I only propose to write a short but comprehensive Essay on Indian Architecture from the materials I may be able to collect; to which I shall perhaps add some descriptions of a few temples and porticoes, principally taken from the Carnatic, with corresponding designs.

"Wishing you and your family every success and prosperity in life,

"I remain,

"Sir,

"Your most obedient and faithful servant,

(Signed) "RAM RAZ."

The Architecture of the Hindus

It is true that the Hindus were in possession of numerous treatises on architecture, sculpture, etc., which collectively are called the *Silpa Sastra,*[1] but unfortunately few traces of them remain. There appears to have been, according to some, thirty-two, and according to others sixty-four, standard treatises on the above-mentioned arts, but of these, excepting a few scattered fragments which are occasionally to be met with among the artists themselves, nothing but the titles of the works are now generally known to the learned. Speaking of these treatises, Sir William Jones expresses it as his opinion that they contained useful information on sixty-four different arts and manufactures; but while I admire his extraordinary talents and extensive knowledge of Asiatic literature, I cannot but think that he was misinformed as to the number of subjects comprised in the *Silpa Sastra,* as from the similarity of the contents of the remains of several of these treatises, and which will be hereafter noticed, there is reason to think that the whole thirty-two, or sixty-four, if there did exist so many, must have treated principally, if not entirely, of sacred architecture and sculpture.

In a series of memorial verses preserved among the artists, are recorded the names of the authors or titles of the above-mentioned sixty-four treatises. Of these, thirty-two are called *Muchya,* or principal, and thirty-two *Upa* or subordinate. I have not been able to ascertain who was the author of these verses, but they contain little more than the titles of the works in question, and which are mostly patronymics of the deities who were believed to have revealed the particular art or arts on which each work treated, or of the authors of the treatises themselves, the renowned *Rishis* or holy men, who are said to have flourished in the earlier ages.

Many works of acknowledged antiquity attest the existence of a number of treatises on *Silpa Sastra*; and every artist proverbially knows that there have been thirty-two principal, and as many subordinate works on this subject. In a Tamil controversial work entitled *Iru-samaya-villacam,* or "the illustration of the two systems," (i.e. of Vishnu and

1. From *silpa,* manual art, and, *sastra,* science. This term, though in its general signification it comprehends the whole of the mechanical arts, is applied commonly, and perhaps by way of pre-eminence, to architecture.

Siva), supposed to have been written in the fifteenth century by a Vaishnava,[1] in refutation of the doctrines of his opponents, or rather in commendation of his own, a work which is held in high estimation, especially among the Vaishnavas in Southern India, the author, in the course of his arguments to prove the supremacy of Vishnu over Siva, has been led incidentally to cite certain passages from the *Silpa Sastra,* which describe the sites to be assigned for the erection of temples for Vishnu and Siva: the former to be in the middle of the town or village, as the most acceptable place for a deity whose characteristic attributes are benignity, mercy, and preservation; and the latter without the village, as proper for one possessed of opposite qualities. This work recognizes a great number of the treatises abovementioned, and enumerates twenty-nine of them by their titles, concluding the list with the words "and others;" but which of these works it was that he consulted on the point of discussion, the author does not inform us: there is reason, however, to believe that many of them had been lost long prior to the period at which he wrote.

Some scattered remains of the treatises entitled *Manasara, Mayamata, Casyapa, Vaikhanasa, Sacaladhicara, Viswacarmiya, Sanatcumara, Saraswatyam, Pancharatram,* and others included in both the lists, are still occasionally, though rarely, to be met with in southern India; and notwithstanding that I have been able to procure considerable portions of the four works first named, and a few detached chapters or sections of each of the rest, it was with considerable difficulty; and unfortunately, the manuscripts which I have collected, are not of a very useful description. Mutilated as they invariably are in many important parts, almost every line of them is not only disfigured by gross errors, perpetuated by a succession of ignorant transcribers, but the technical terms and memorial verses with which the whole abounds, are so little understood either by the artists or the pundits of the present day that it requires no ordinary exertion to comprehend and explain the exact import of even a single section.

The first work, entitled *Manasara,* is the most perfect I have seen, and perhaps the most perfect on the subject that now exists. It is stated to be the production of a sage named Manasara and is of great celebrity in the south of India, as affording copious information on every branch of the art on which he treats, but particularly on that of building sacred edifices; and it is often consulted by the artists as the highest authority for the solution of contested points in architecture. This work appears, according to an enumeration of the contents given in the preface, to consist of fifty-eight *adhyayas* or chapters,[2] each of which is devoted to a particular topic; but the portion I have in my possession contains no more than forty-one chapters, in which are described the measures used in architecture, sculpture, etc; the different sites to be selected for building temples and houses; the mode of determining the different points of the compass; the several

1. A follower of Vishnu.
2. In order that a more accurate idea may be formed of the subjects contained in this work, a particular description is given of the contents of each *adhyaya* as taken from the preface. The first chapter treats of the measures used in architecture, sculpture, carpentry, etc.; the second describes the qualification of a *Silpi,* and gives a brief account of the origin of the five different classes of artists, said to have been descended from *Viswacarma,* and to have followed respectively the occupations of sculptors, joiners, braziers, jewellers, and blacksmiths. The third, fourth, and

sorts of villages, towns, and cities, with directions for building them; the different parts of an edifice, its ornaments, pedestals, bases, pillars, entablatures, etc.; the various sorts of temples, consisting of from one to twelve storeys high; the construction of *mandapas* or porticoes, gates, and doorways, palaces, etc. The remainder of the work appears to contain ample information respecting the whole process in the construction of images, and of cars and other vehicles in which the gods are carried in procession; but these subjects are more immediately connected with sculpture and carpentry than with architecture. It may be proper to notice, however, that a considerable portion of the whole is occupied

---

fifth chapters explain the nature and qualities of the soil on which buildings should be erected, such as temples, palaces, and private dwelling-houses for the several classes of people. The sixth contains rules and directions for constructing a gnomon, for the purpose of determining the several points of the compass. The seventh treats of the parts into which the ground-plan of the cities, towns, temples, palaces and houses should be divided. The eighth chapter gives a minute description of sacrifices and other devotional rites to be performed on various occasions in the building of temples, houses, etc. The ninth chapter treats of villages and towns, and prescribes rules for the formation of streets, and the allotment of fit places for the erection of temples, and for the residence of the different classes of people. The tenth contains a description of the different sorts of cities; the eleventh treats of the dimensions of the several sorts of edifices; the twelfth of the *Garbhatvinyasa,* or laying the foundation-stone in the centre of the intended building; the thirteenth of *Upapithas* or pedestals; the fourteenth of *Adhisthana* or basement; the fifteenth of the several species of pillars, with their respective dimensions; the sixteenth of *Prastaras,* or entablature, the seventeenth of the junction of the several parts of timber work, with reference to their points; the eighteenth of *Vimanas,* temples, or palaces in general. Twelve successive chapters, from the nineteenth to the twenty-eighth, contain descriptions of temples surmounted by pyramidal domes, consisting of from one to twelve storeys, with their respective dimensions. The twenty-ninth chapter treats of *Pracaras* or outer courts of temples; the thirtieth of the attendant deities, and the parts respectively assigned to each within the walls of the temple; the thirty-first of *Gopuras* or pyramidal buildings, or turrets raised over the gateways leading into the temples; the thirty-second of *Mandapas,* or porticoes, or resting-places for the deity; the thirty-third of *Salas* or halls; the thirty-fourth of cities; the thirty-fifth of private dwelling-houses; the thirty-sixth and thirty-seventh of gates and doorways, with their dimensions; the thirty-eighth and thirty-ninth of the palaces and their appendages; the fortieth of princes with their titles; the forty-first of the building of cars and other vehicles of the gods; the forty-second of couches, cushions, and the like; the forty-third of the thrones for the gods and for princes; the forty-fourth of ornamental arches; the forty-fifth of the *Calpataru,* or the all-productive tree, which is supposed to be planted in Indra's heaven, and to supply all the wants of those who have the happiness of taking shelter under it. The forty-sixth chapter treats of *Abhishecas,* or ablutionary rites, by which images are sanctified; the forty-seventh of jewels and ornaments worn by the gods and mortals; the forty-eighth of statues of Brahma and other deities; the forty-ninth of the *Lingam*—the emblem of Siva; the fiftieth of seats and forms raised for the reception of images; the fifty-first of the form of *Sakti*—the goddess of nature; the fifty-second and fifty-third of the images worshipped by the Bauddhas and Jainas; the fifty-fourth describes the statues of *Yacshas, Vidyadharas,* and other choristers; the fifty-fifth those of the saints or holy men; the fifty-sixth and fifty-seventh those of the Devas or gods, with their respective vehicles; and the fifty-eighth concludes with rules for chiselling the eyes of the statue, and the ceremonies to be performed on the occasion.

with a minute description of the mysteries, rites, and sacrifices to be performed on various occasions, in the building of temples, houses, villages, towns, and cities; the ceremonies attending the consecration of images; the mode of determining the propitious moment for commencing to lay the foundation of an edifice, as well as rules for predicting the future prosperity of him who causes the edifice to be raised, by the aspect of the stars, the situation of the building with respect to the cardinal points, and other astrological devices.

The second work, entitled *Mayamata,* is ascribed to Maya,[1] probably the author or compiler of the *Suryasiddhanta,* a work on astronomy of the greatest repute, and who is stated in the *Ramayana* of Valmiki to have prepared the altar for the sacrifice performed by Dasaratha, the king of Ayodhya (Oude), and father of Rama. It differs little from the *Manasara* in the main arrangement of the subjects. It opens with the mystical rites performed in honour of the *Vastu,* or the spirit presiding over the ground on which buildings are erected, and proceeds to give rules for the examination of the soil, the preparation of it for buildings in general, the construction of a gnomon for the purpose of determining the cardinal points, the division of the ground-plan into several parts for religious as well as domestic purposes, and the performance of sacrifices previous to the commencement of the work; after which it describes the several sorts of villages, cities, and fortresses, *upapithas* or pedestals, the *adhisthanas* or bases, the *padas* or pillars, the *prastaras* or entablatures, the ornaments used in cavettos under the cupola, the seats raised for the reception of idols, the *sicharas* or the domes of temples, the ceremonies observed in laying the first and the last stone of an edifice, the several sorts of temples, the courts by which they are surrounded, the pyramidal gateways, the *mandapas* or porticoes, the altars to be raised in the front of temples, and concludes with instructions for the carving of images, etc.

The third work, entitled *Casyapa,* is attributed to the sage whose name it bears, a personage celebrated in sacred writings of great antiquity. He is considered as one of the progenitors of mankind, and ranked the first amongst the seven holy men who were preserved from the universal deluge, and who peopled the earth soon after that great event. This treatise, though more succinct than the former two, contains sufficient information on the subject of sacred architecture and sculpture; the whole is composed in a dramatic form, and is stated in the preface to have been revealed to the author personally by Siva; and in consequence, the former is frequently addressed throughout the book by the appellation of *Dwijottama,* "the best of the twice-born," and the like. The subjects contained in this work are nearly the same as those contained in the *Manasara,* but the arrangement is somewhat different. It commences with the description of the several sorts of soil which are considered proper for buildings, and proceeds to the

1. Maya is also stated in the *Mahabharata* to have erected a splendid palace for the residence of the five sons of *Pandu,* a poetical description of which occupies a whole book of that celebrated work. He is supposed to be one and the same person with him who erected the altar for Dasaratha, and the seeming inconsistency of his being contemporary with *Rama* and *Krishna,* in two such remote periods as the *Creta* and *Dwapara Yugas,* mythological writers reconcile by assigning a supernatural term to the life of the personage in question.

preparatory rites and sacrifices to be performed in honour of the *Vastupurusha,* or the spirit presiding over the ground appropriate for the erecting of temples and houses; thence to the mode of constructing a *sanchu* or gnomon for the purpose of ascertaining the points of the compass, and thence to the laying of the foundation-stone, and the ceremonies to be observed on this occasion. It afterwards describes the pedestals, the bases, the gates of the temples, and doorways of houses, pillars, capitals, and other ornaments; the seats raised on the pavements of temples, and niches for the reception of images; aqueducts or water-courses; the several sorts of *vimanas* or shrines with the pyramidal towers, consisting of from one to sixteen storeys; the *toranas* or ornamental arches erected over gateways and pillars; doors and their dimensions; statues of the gods, saints, and holy men, etc.

The fourth treatise, called *Vaikhanasa,* is the work of a sage so named, and who was the founder of a sect of Vaishnava priests. It is written in a sort of metrical prose, and is rather ritual than architectural; and as the author in the latter part of the work frequently cites the authority of *Casyapa,* and as the work itself is included among the subordinate treatises enumerated in the list, it appears to be comparatively a modern performance. It opens with an encomium on the land of Bharata,[1] as being peculiarly sacred, and adapted for the performance of holy rites and sacrifices; and thence proceeds to describe the various sacrifices ordained in the Veda, to be performed when the purpose is to obtain special boons or favours, either temporal or spiritual, such as progeny, riches, wisdom, absolution from sin, purification, etc. It next treats of the mystical rites practised in honour of Vastu, preparatory to the building of sacred edifices, or of altars for sacrifices; of villages, towns, and cities, the fruits to be derived from building and peopling them with Brahmans; the construction of temples dedicated to Vishnu, with rules for carving the images of that deity and his attendants, on whose attributes the author occasionally dwells with that devotion and zeal which characterize all his followers.

The work entitled *Sacaladhicara,* an excellent but rather voluminous performance, is attributed to Agastya, a sage whose history occupies a conspicuous place in the Puranas. Some few sections only of this work are to be now met with; and the portion which has as yet come under my own observation, is exclusively on the subject of sculpture as connected with the formation of statues; but it is so diffuse, that if we suppose the whole work to be written in a similar style, it must considerably exceed the volume of *Manasara,* the largest at present of my collection.

As I have but a few detached pieces of the other works mentioned above, they do not appear to call for any distinct notice. Some of these pieces are descriptive of the construction of temples, some of the towers over gateways, some contain directions for laying the foundation of a building, some treat of the auspicious and inauspicious seasons for the commencement of an edifice, and others of the manufacture of images and so forth. However, as the rules contained in these fragments differ very little in substance from those laid down in the *Manasara* and other treatises on the same subject, I shall seldom have occasion to refer to them in the course of this essay.

---

1. India.

The exact age of each of these treatises it is very difficult to ascertain. Tradition gives to most of them an antiquity altogether extravagant; and however diligent the endeavour to obtain authentic information on this point, success can hardly be expected to attend it, when we consider in what obscurity and oblivion the ancient history and chronology of the Hindus are involved. Of Manasara,[1] the sage to whom the first treatise is attributed, I have not been able to procure any distinct historical notice; but, as has already been mentioned, the supposed authors of the other treatises, entitled *Casyapa* and *Mayamata*, are, under these names, greatly celebrated in the Puranas and other sacred writings of antiquity. That all these treatises were composed in the south of India, there appears indeed no reason to doubt, for they seem to have been the standards by which the existing religious structures were reared throughout this part of the peninsula.

The most interesting circumstance connected with these treatises is their toleration of the worship of the Jainas and Bauddhas, the authors of them having carefully pointed out distinct sites to be set apart in villages and towns for the erecting of their temples, and having likewise prescribed rules for constructing images of the objects of adoration by these sects. This prescription marks, though indefinitely, the age of these compositions to have been posterior to the great schism, which took place between the Hindus and Jains, and which terminated in the overthrow of the latter. The contentment, too, of this latter sect with the inferior situation assigned them by their conquerors for their divine worship, in a place contiguous to that which, among Hindus, is usually appropriated to the shrines of inferior deities and malignant spirits, evinces their complete subordination at the period alluded to.

Another circumstance in that portion of the foregoing treatises which has fallen into my hands is worthy of notice. They prove by internal evidence that they were written at a period subsequent to the canonization of Apper, Sundarer, Sammander, Manicyavasarer, and other holy men, several of whom are supposed to have lived between the third and fifth century of *Salivahn*. The ground on which this proof rests is that in the chapters which prescribe rules for carving statues, directions are likewise given for carving those of the personages here mentioned, who have been admitted among the inferior divinities, and assumed their places around, the temple of Siva, particularly in the south of India. But some learned men to whom I mentioned this circumstance, rather than concur in an opinion which detracts from the antiquity of these works, are inclined to think that the passages in question are modem interpolations.

The small portion which has come under my observation of the work called *Sacaladhicara*, "the universal authority," does not furnish sufficient data to form any opinion of the precise time at which it was composed; and in the section which gives rules for carving statues, that is, in the only part I have seen of it, I find no mention of the saints above referred to. It is generally believed to have been composed by Agastya, under the auspices of the founder of the Pandya government, a circumstance which, if

1. Some say Manasara is not the name of the author but the title of the work itself, signifying "the essence of proportion," and which, from this etymology, I am inclined to believe; but whatever may be the real name of the author, I shall make use of the word both as the name of the author and the title of the work throughout this essay.

admitted, would give to this work a very high antiquity. It is, however, difficult to trace the exact period when the Pandya principality was originally established. Mr. Wilson, in his prefatory remarks to his catalogue of the M'Kenzie collection, places this event three or four centuries before the Christian era, although in another place he fixes the date of the civilization of the south of India, ten centuries before Christ; but the data on which this conjecture is formed is imperfect, being derived from a source which can be no authority 'in matters of this nature.[1] There exists indeed a long list of the princes of the Pandya, and their contemporary Chola and Chera dynasties, many of whom appear to have reigned long anterior to the Christian era, and their celebrity to have attracted the notice of Ptolemy. The few facts, it is true, that have been recorded of these dynasties, or preserved by tradition, are unfortunately inadequate to the formation of a connected sketch of their history, or to trace their chronology with precision; but the various accounts, which are obtainable of these ancient monarchies, though, they usually commence with the earliest ages, and are blended with marvellous and extravagant fictions, would still afford ample historical proofs of the establishment of these principalities at an earlier period than what has been hitherto assigned them by western antiquarians. And as the *Mahabharata,* which is believed to have been composed by Vyasa, in the beginning of the Kaliyug, makes mention of the Pandya and Chola governments, we must give them credit for a higher antiquity.

That the religion and literature, as well as the political constitution of the South, were derived from the North, the earliest seat of the Hindu empire as well as of arts and sciences, and that the southern peninsula was before that period a vast uncultivated forest, inhabited by small insulated tribes, speaking a jargon which hardly furnished them with terms expressive of their immediate and natural wants, there is scarcely any doubt. While in this state of society, the sage Agastya, to whom the treatise under examination is attributed, appears to have brought hither the first colony of Brahmans and other classes from the north, and with them the Hindu religion and literature, in form the same as at the present day. He is believed to have been the inventor of the letters now in use in the Tamil, and the first who refined that language on the principles of the Sanskrit or northern dialect; and as this personage is stated also to have officiated both as minister and spiritual teacher to the founder of the Pandya principality, it is not unlikely, that the usefulness of the art of building to such an infant state, should have induced him to write a treatise on the subject.

The foregoing notice of the contents of the several treatises, or fragments of treatises, may seem to promise a good deal of useful information on the arts of which they treat; but, in truth, the architectural portions of them, if divested of all the extraneous matter with which they abound, contain little more than a dry detail of the technical names and of the proportions of the several members of a sacred edifice. It has already been stated that considerable portions of the works mentioned above are replete with minute descriptions of religious rites, to be performed on various occasions from the

1. The author, it would appear, identifies the civilization of the South of India with the establishment of the Pandya principality; events which Professor Wilson conjectures, on the authority of the traditional records of the South, to be distinct, and of different eras.

commencement, to the completion of a building as well as rules and aphorisms drawn from its situation, aspect, etc. for predicting the future destiny of the builder. The latter, however, form no part of the present inquiry, and they are interesting so far only as being descriptive of the customs of the ancient Hindus, with regard to their belief in divinations, omens, prodigies, etc., a belief which is still fondly adhered to by their posterity. With respect to other branches of the art on which information is wanting, it is stated by good authorities, and there is reason to believe the statement, that military architecture is treated of at length in some of the ancient treatises on *Arthasastra,* or political science, and particularly in one attributed to Chanakya, the well-known minister of Chandragupta.[1] The same authorities also state that ample instruction for the building of private dwelling-houses is contained in other works, professedly written on civil architecture.[2] However, as these books are not at present to be met with, it has been thought advisable to restrict this research to religious architecture.

I now proceed to a more detailed consideration of the portions of the treatises in my possession, trusting that it may serve to elucidate both the theory and practice of the art. In doing this, I propose occasionally to introduce extracts from the authorities which I may consult, and to make my own observations regarding any affinity which to me may seem to exist between the Indian and European systems.

The first chapter of the *Manasara* treats of the several measurements used in architecture, sculpture, etc. In measuring space, the Hindus commonly take their reckoning from the most minute quantity or extent; and Manasara, like others who have treated on the subject, begins his measure from *paramanu,* which he defines to be the particle perceptible only to the eyes of the sages, perhaps thereby importing the atoms spoken of in the writings of philosophers, while others have identified it with one of those subtle particles of substance, which are seen floating in the reflected light of a sun-beam. 'Eight' of these *paramanus* make one *ratharenu,* or grain of dust raised up by the wheels of carriages; eight *ratharenu,* one *valagra,* the point of a hair; eight *valagras* are equal in size to a louse; eight lice to a grain of *yava*; three, three and a half, and four *yavas* make one *angula,* or finger of the inferior, middle, and superior sorts respectively. Twelve *angulas* make one *vitasti* or span; two *vitastis* one *hasta* or cubit, which is equal to twenty-four *angulas,* and is sometimes called *cishcu hasta,* lesser cubit, in contra-distinction to *prajapatya hasta,* which is equal to twenty-five *angulas*. Twenty-six *angulas* make one *dhanurmushti,* or the grasp of a bow; twenty-seven *angulas,* one *dhanurgraha* or the handle of a bow. Thus, the *hastas* are fourfold; the first or *cishcu* is employed in the construction of couches, vehicles, and the like; the second or *prajapatya* is used in building temples, pyramids, etc.; the third or *dhanurmushti* in constructing houses; and the fourth or *dhanurgraha,* in the measurement of villages, towns, and cities. According to some,

1. A celebrated prince, who reigned in Pataliputra when Alexander visited the upper Hindustan; the same who is known to the Greek writers by the name of Sandracottus.
2. Since writing the above, a respectable friend of mine had the kindness to procure me, from Travancore, a copy of a work entitled *Manushyalaya Chandrica,* which, as its name implies, treats of that branch of the art which applies to private houses, but of the description built in that kingdom.

however, the *cishcu hasta* is adopted for all these purposes indiscriminately. Again, four *hastas* make one *danda* or staff, which is sometimes called *yesti,* and sometimes *dhanus;* and eight *dandas* are equal to one *rajju,* a cord which is employed in measuring all sorts of land. In raising sacrificial altars, a particular sort of *angula* is used, equal in size to the intermediate space between the two middle joints of the middle finger of the *carta,* or master, and which is thence called *matrangula.*

The second chapter of the *Manasara* treats of the qualities of an architect (*Silpi lacshanam*); and as preliminary thereto, of the origin of artists of the several kinds, and which is traced to *Viswacarma* the heavenly architect. This personage is stated to have had four heads, probably in allusion to the supernatural talents with which he was endowed, and to his invention of so many useful arts. Another *Viswacarma, Twashtri, Maya,* and *Manu* are named as his sons, and said to have left four other offspring, whose names, however, are not mentioned in any of the works under examination, but of whom the first is affirmed to have been by profession a *sthapati,* architect; the second *sutragrahi,* the measurer; the third *vardhaci,* the joiner; and the last *tacshaca,* the carpenter; and all of whom are considered as indispensably necessary to the building of an edifice. Their intermarriage, also, with the families of some noted persons of the Hindu mythology, is adverted to as a further proof of the divine origin of the artists; and the whole concludes with a short notice of their requisite qualifications, of which the following passages from the *Manushyalaya Chandrica*[1] will convey some idea.

> An architect *(sthapati)* should be conversant in all sciences; ever attentive to his avocations; of an unblemished character; generous, sincere, and devoid of enmity or jealousy.
>
> Of nearly equal qualification with him should be the *sutragrahi;* he may be either the son or disciple of the *sthapati;* he should be particularly skilled in mathematics, and be strictly obedient to the will of the *sthapati.*
>
> A *tacshaca,* who is thus called from part of his avocation being to pare the rough wood, should be of a cheerful temper, and well versed in all mechanical arts.
>
> A *vardhaci* is he who is dexterous in joining wood, and uniting other materials one with another; he should be of a calm disposition, and acquainted with drawing and perspective.
>
> As it is impossible to build houses and the like without the aid of the four descriptions of artisans, *sthapati* and so forth, let the enlightened twice-born[2] gratify them in every respect, so that buildings may be erected.
>
> Woe to them who dwell in a house not built according to the proportions of symmetry. In building an edifice, therefore, let all its parts, from the basement to the roof, be duly considered.

The word *sthapati* is from *stha,* that which is fixed or formed, and *pati,* lord or master, and consequently, like the Greek **Αρχιτεκτων**, signifies a person who presides over the erecting of an edifice, the formation of a statue, and the construction of a chariot, etc.

1. A treatise on civil architecture referred to in the preceding note.
2. Brahmans, Cshetriyas, Vaisyas, or men of the first, second or third classes.

The principal qualifications of an architect consist in a knowledge of various branches of learning, such as arithmetic, geometry, drawing, sculpture, mythology, astrology, etc., the usefulness of all of which to a master-builder is too obvious to require any comment. Nor are these qualifications altogether unlike those which Vitruvius and other western architects have prescribed as indispensable to their profession, if we except the knowledge of medicine, music, and even anatomy, which the latter have thought proper to add to the qualifications of an architect. It is curious to observe that among other moral qualities enumerated in the texts cited above, as requisite in the Hindu architect, is included 'sincerity,' a virtue, the want of which in the artists of India is proverbial.

The third chapter of the *Manasara* professes to treat of the nature and qualities of the ground on which buildings are to be erected. It opens with the definition of *vastu*, a term used to express the ground on which any superstructure is raised, as signifying that which is inhabitable, and directs a careful examination of the site to be selected for building, as to its fitness for the purpose from its colour, smell, taste, form, and touch. It then goes on to divide the soil into four sorts, and to point out in the order of superiority what is considered auspicious for the residence of each of the four classes, with reference to the five qualities above-mentioned. Nay, some have gone even so far as to forbid the lower class from occupying the ground suited to the higher, and vice versa, on pain of incurring the severest vengeance of heaven; but the principle on which these distinctions are founded is altogether nugatory. It signifies little whether the ground designed for the residence of a Brahman be square or oblong, white or red, sweet or sour, provided that the situation is convenient, and that it furnishes a firm bottom for laying the foundation; nor is it possible to find a place possessing all the qualities required by this prescription for the residence of anyone of the classes; and, in order perhaps to obviate this difficulty, another more general classification of the soil into three sorts is added, with a declaration that the first two will answer the purposes of all classes of men without exception.

> The best sort of ground should abound with milky[1] trees, full of fruits and flowers; its boundary should be of a quadrangular form, level and smooth, with a sloping declivity towards the east, producing a hard sound, with a stream running from left to right, of an agreeable odour, fertile, of an uniform colour, containing a great quantity of soil, producing water when dug to the height of a man's arm raised above his head, and situated in a climate of moderate temperature. The ground possessed of qualities directly opposite to those mentioned above is the worst, and that which has a mixed nature is the middling.

The ground to be avoided is described in a special manner as follows:

> That which has the form of a circle, a semicircle, containing three, five, or six angles, resembling a trident or a winnow, shaped like the hinder part of a fish, or the back of an elephant, or a turtle, or the face of a cow, and the like; situated opposite to any of the intermediate quarters north-west, and the like; abounding with human sculls, stones,

1. Chadira (*mimosa* of Linn.), cadumba (*naseclea*), nimba (*margosa*), champaca (*michelia*), punnaga (*mesua* of Linn.), amlaca (*emblica* of Linn.), patala (*bignonia*), saptaparna (*echites* of Linn.), and some others, belong to this species of trees.

> worms, ant-hills, bones, slimy earth, decayed woods, coals, dilapidated wells, subterraneous pits, fragments of tiles, lime-stones, ashes, husks of corn; and exposed to the wafted effluvia of curds, oil, honey, dead bodies, fishes, etc.: such a spot should be avoided on every account.

The following rule is laid down in the first section of the *Casyapa,* for the purpose of ascertaining the solidity of the ground on which the foundation is to be laid. "Having dug a pit a *hasta* in depth, in the middle of the ground, return the earth into it, and according to the space which the latter may now take up with reference to that which it occupied before the digging of the pit, whether more, less, or the same, the ground should be considered as good, bad, or indifferent; the good and indifferent sorts are acceptable, but the bad should by all means be avoided."

After the ground has been chosen with due regard to its qualities, the *sthapati,* in an auspicious moment, must cause the rites of purification to be performed, the prescribed oblations made, and consecrated water to be sprinkled on all sides, accompanied with invocations for the prosperity of the builder. The soil is then ploughed and certain ceremonies prescribed for this occasion are also observed.

The fourth chapter of the *Manasara* contains rules for the construction of the plough, and directions for ploughing the ground, preparatory to erecting temples, etc.

> A plough,

says the author,

> must be made of the *chadira,*[1] *nimba,*[2] or of the wood of any other milky tree. It must be from one to one and a half *hasta* in length, with a tapering point resembling the leaf of a *bambu,* furnished with a share of three, five, or six *angulas* long and two thick, and with a beam of three yards in length. This machine is to be yoked to a pair of oxen of equal size and of the same colour, either white, black, red, or gray. The oxen should be strong, and such as have not exceeded the middle age. Oxen with horns bent down, maimed, weak, meagre, toothless, or lame, should be rejected; those with a white spot on their legs and foreheads, with eyes resembling the petals of the lotus, are to be preferred. They should be decorated with fillets and the like, and their horns and hoofs with gold or silver rings. The *sthapati,* clad in fresh garments, and adorned with garlands of flowers, waits the auspicious moment to present his offerings to the deity, and then, guiding the oxen, draws the first furrow. After this, *sudras,*[3] hired for the purpose, complete the ploughing of the whole ground.

A minuter description of the plough is contained in the first section of the *Casyapa,* the insertion of which may not be irrelevant in this place as affording some proof that, how rude soever this useful implement of the Hindu husbandmen of the present day may appear, it has been originally constructed on principles derived from no slight knowledge of mechanical laws. The author says,

> the plough should be made from the wood of any species of milky trees, such as are used in sacrifices, and according to the prescribed form; let the beam be three *hastas* long, with a

---

1. *Mimosa* of Linn.
2. *Margosa.*
3. Men of the fourth class.

> projection of seven *angulas* from the yoke, and its bottom six *angulas* broad, four thick, tapering gradually from the lower to the higher end, with a slight indenture about the middle. The inverted piece at the lower end of the stilt or handle should be nine *angulas* long, two broad, and one and a half thick. The mould-board should be twenty-four *angulas* long, and its height above the beam, five. Let a head be fashioned in the bosom of the mould-board, of fourteen *angulas* in length, and the remainder of the inverted piece may be said to be taken up by the hole in which the beam and the handle are joined together. Let the mould-board be six *angulas* broad and four thick, with a point shaped like a pin, and gradually diminished towards the front; three times five *angulas* are said to be the interval between the beam and the fore end of the mould-board, to which the coulter should be fixed; the yoke pole is equal in length to the beam, with holes at both ends, and a leathern strap attached to each, of two *hastas* in length, and of the thickness of the little finger.

> Having yoked the oxen,

continues the same author,

> a little more to the right than to the left of the pole, or towards the right hand of the driver, and having recited the appropriate prayers, let furrows be drawn towards the east or west, the grass being plucked out in the first instance. Let sesamum seeds, pulse, and kidney-beans be sown, with incantations pronounced over them, and let due reverence be paid to the spiritual teacher, and the oxen and the plough to which they are attached presented to him. When the crops are matured, and the flowers in bloom, let them be grazed on by cattle, and let cows remain on them for one or two nights. The ground will become purified by the froth flowing from the mouths of the cows, and by their ordure, after which you may commence building in the centre thereof.

The next thing of seeming importance treated of by Hindu architects, is the mode of ascertaining the cardinal points by means of a gnomon. It is indispensably necessary that all the quarters should be distinctly and precisely marked on the spot on which buildings are to be erected, for the purpose of giving them an auspicious aspect, and of preventing their being opposite to any of the intermediate points, which are declared to be inauspicious. The sixth chapter of the *Manasara* is exclusively devoted to this subject, the fifth containing directions for performing certain religious rites to propitiate the presiding deities of the soil. The first section of the *Casyapa* combines both these topics, and the fifth of the *Mayamata* corresponds with the sixth of the *Manasara*; but the portions of the manuscripts which are in my possession are so imperfect from the causes before noticed that the whole, taken together, conveys but a very imperfect idea of the subject treated on, and recourse has therefore been had to other sources to supply the defect.

The mode of ascertaining the points of the compass by the shadow of a gnomon is extremely simple. "On a smooth level piece of ground is erected a gnomon," which according to some, "should be of sixteen *angulas* in height, and of the same diameter at the bottom; the whole should be shaped like the leaf of an opening bud, tapering gradually from the bottom to the top."

> Around this a circle is drawn with a cord of twice the height of the gnomon, by fixing one end of it to its base and carrying the other around it. Points are marked in the circumference where the shadow of the gnomon projects, both in the forenoon and afternoon, that is at any given hour after sun-rise, and at the same time before sun-set; and between these points a right line is drawn so as to join them; the point marked by the morning shadow will show the east, and that marked by the evening shadow the west. Then, from each of

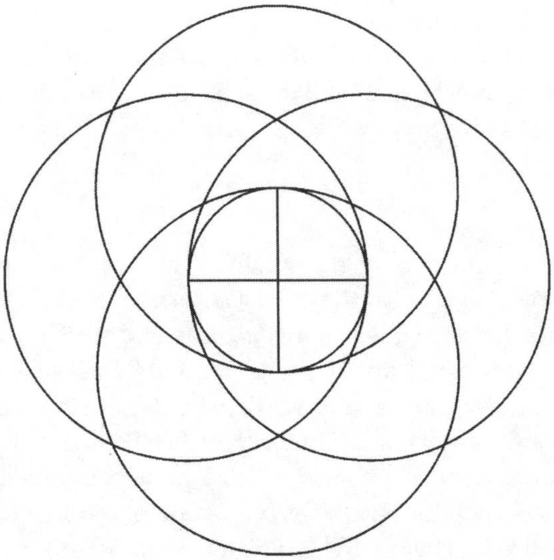

> these two points, and with a radius equal to the distance between them, describe two more circles cutting each other, and resembling (in their points of intersection) the head and tail of a fish, between which draw a right line, which will point to the south and north. Again, from the southern and northern points which touch the circumference of the inner circle respectively, and with the same radius, describe two more circles, and the points of intersection on the two other sides will indicate the east and west.

The text goes on with repeating a similar process for ascertaining the intermediate points. Some treatises require the first circle to be described around the gnomon, not previous to making the morning and afternoon shadows, but afterwards; and in this case, the shadow being marked in the first instance, the circle is described from the centre of the gnomon, with a radius equal to the length of the shadow, plus half the diameter of the gnomon.

Various rules have been laid down for the purpose of rectifying the variation of the shadow owing to the irregularity of the sun's motion in the ecliptic, the simplest of which seems to be as follows: The place where the shadow of the gnomon projects, on two successive days at the same hour, being marked, the difference between those two days, is taken as the variation of the shadow for sixty *ghaticas* or twenty-four hours. The interval between the times at which the western and eastern points were marked on the preceding day is multiplied by the difference of the shadow measured for one day, and the product being divided by sixty *ghaticas,* the result will give the difference of the shadow for the given time; it will then be only necessary to remove the eastern or western point so far towards the south or north, according as the difference of the shadow on the second day may be in either of those directions, or as the sun is in the southern or northern solstice.

Another rule for finding the true points is given in the *Surya Siddhanta.*

> But, in consequence of the processional variation of the times of the shadow marked in the east and west of the circle, the difference in the sine of the declination between those times, being multiplied by the hypotenuse of the shadow at either of those times, and the product divided by the cosine of the latitude, the quotient will give the *angulas*; remove the western

point so many *angulas* in the opposite quarter of the sun's declination, and the eastern point will become due east; or else, according as the sun is in the northern or southern solstice, the eastern point may be removed the same distance in that direction.

Having marked,

says the commentary,

a point in the middle of a level piece of ground, from that point, and with a radius equal to the length of the shadow projected at the third *ghatica* after the sun's rise, plus half of the diameter of the gnomon (because the shadow is measured from the circumference of the gnomon), let a circle be described, and in the centre of it let a *sanchu* be erected, of twelve *angulas* in height and of the same diameter: mark points where the shadow falls before and after noon on the east and west of the circumference; then having computed the sines of the declination three *ghaticas* after sun-rise, and three *ghaticas* before sun-set, multiply the difference between these two sines by the hypothenuse of the shadow at the third *ghatica* after sun-rise, and the product being divided by the cosine of the latitude of the place, the quotient will give the *anguku* or their integral parts. Then remove the eastern point so many *angulas,* etc. according as the sun is in the south or north latitude; by this means all the points of the compass may be rectified.

Passing over several sections of the *Manasara,* which are not immediately connected with the main purpose of this essay, and reserving one or two of them for future consideration, we now come to the thirteenth and fourteenth, which treat of pedestals and bases.

The Hindu orders may be said to consist of four principal parts, namely, the *upapitha* or pedestal, the *athisthana* or base, the *sthamba* or pillar and the *prastara* or entablature. Western architects consider the base not as a distinct member, but as a constituent part of the column; and this is not altogether at variance with the practice of the Hindu architects, for they likewise include the base and capital in taking the height of the pillar, and even consider the pedestal as a necessary part of the order. However, the latter invariably treat of a pedestal and base as separate bodies, as they are sometimes employed without pillars. These several members of the order have also been subdivided into various inferior parts, and the whole are curiously compared to the several parts of the human body, in all which particulars a striking similarity may be perceived between the Indian and European systems.

The two first members now under consideration derive their names as *upapitha* and *athisthana*—the former from *upa,* under, and *pitha,* a seat or bench, and the latter from *adhi,* upon, and *stka,* to stand. Both are for the most part composed of the same mouldings; but the most remarkable feature in which they differ is the square dye, which is peculiar to the former. The pedestal is not only placed under the base of a column or pilaster, but frequently employed, both singly and together with the latter, as a pavement for temples and porticoes, over cornices of edifices consisting of several storeys in height, and also as a platform for thrones, and as seats for statues. In the latter situations especially, their decorations will be found to have employed much of the skill of the Hindu artists, and the most finished specimens of them may be justly said to surpass anything of the kind in the Grecian or Roman orders, both in the beauty of their proportions and richness of their ornaments.

The several mouldings which enter into the composition of pedestals and bases are: 1. *upana,* 2. *campa;* 3. *gala, cantha, griva,* or *candhara;* 4. *uttara;* 5. *vajina;* 6. *prativajina;* 7. *pattica;* 8. *alinga;* and 9. *antarita,* all of which are of a quadrangular form, and 10. *cumuda;* 11. *padma;* 12. *capota,* etc., which are circular. And as these mouldings frequently occur in the description of the several sorts of pedestals and bases which will be presently exhibited, a brief notice of their respective forms and uses, as well as of their correspondence with the mouldings of similar members in western architecture, may not be a useless preliminary, especially, as it may tend to the disclosure of any mistakes into which I may have fallen, in identifying the mouldings described in books, with those found in the existing models of the art, the technical terms above-mentioned being no longer in use (See Plate I).

To begin, then, with the circular mouldings: the section of that which is called *cumuda* (10), literally *nymphaea esculenta,* is a semicircle projecting from a vertical diameter, and corresponds with the astragal, bead, or torus of the Grecian orders. It is chiefly employed in bases and cornices.

The moulding called *padma,* (11) literally lotus, is supposed to resemble a petal of that flower. It is a sort of compound figure, partly convex and partly concave; and its section is composed of two opposite curves, meeting at the bisecting point of a line drawn between the points of recess and projection, and very much resembling the *cima recta* and *reversa* of the western architects. This moulding is distinguished into greater and less, and forms the principal ornaments of Indian architecture. It is generally employed in detached pairs, in bases and cornices, one facing the other in opposite directions, and is formed upright or the reverse according to its situation, either as a crowning member of the former or the supporting ornament of the latter. The concave part of it, when placed with its bottom reversed, is often so designed as to project forward or rise up, after having touched, as it were, the fillet below, with a small perpendicular curvature, resembling in shape the petal of the lotus, with its pointed head somewhat inclined towards the top. In some specimens, this moulding is placed at the base of columns, and looks very much like an *apophyge* or ogre of the Ionic and Corinthian orders, being formed either with a curved line having more or less convexity at the top, or with an upright tangent to the concave part below. It is sometimes made exactly in the form of an ovolo of the western architects.

A *capotam* (12) is a section of moulding made in the form of a pigeon's head, from which it takes its name. It is a crowning member of cornices, pedestals, and entablatures. When employed in the latter, it often connects utility with beauty, in as much as the beak of the bird is so placed as to serve the purpose of a spout to throw off the water falling on the cornice. In this office it resembles, in some measure, the *corona* or the Grecian order.

The square members above-mentioned are nothing more than rectangular figures or parallelograms, differing from one another only in their degrees of altitude and projection. Of all the rectangular mouldings, a *campa* (2) has the least height, and its projection, though generally equal to its altitude, frequently varies according to the position of the principal members, which it is employed to connect or to separate; and it answers, in every respect, to the fillet or *listel* of the western architects.

An *upana* (1) corresponds exactly with the plinth, both in the import of the term and the purpose to which it is applied.

A *cantha, gala* or *griva,* etc. (3) literally means the neck; and when employed in pedestals, it is made very high, and resembles the *dado,* but everywhere else it serves as a sort of neutral member, from which the projections of the rest of the mouldings are measured.

A *vajina* (5) is distinguished from the *campa,* by the former having a greater projection than the latter.

A *prativajina* (6) is the same thing made in pedestals to answer to the *vajina*; its form, though generally rectangular, is sometimes, when placed in cornices, found to be externally a little more inclined to one side than to the other; and in this situation it very much resembles the *cavetto.*

A *patta* or *pattica* (7) signifies a band. It is often confounded with the moulding called *vajina,* especially in pedestals and bases, as it appears to be of the same form, to be used in the same situation, and to have the same height and projection with the latter; but when employed in architraves and friezes, its height and projection increase considerably.

An *uttara* (4) is used sometimes to signify the whole architrave, and sometimes to denote a particular member of the pedestal and entablature, called by the western architects *corona.*

An *alinga* (8) generally has the same altitude with the fillet, but a greater projection than it.

An *antarita* (9) has the same height with the *alinga,* but as much recession as the latter has projection. Both these members are placed alternately together and, when used, are always thus inseparably connected.

OF PEDESTALS

Hindu architects have invariably taken the dimensions of their pedestals from those of the bases to which they are attached; but as to the number of parts to be given to the height of pedestals, with reference to the number of parts contained in the base, there exists a multiplicity of contradictory rules. On this subject Manasara, our principal guide, expresses himself in so obscure a manner that I must acknowledge my inability to understand him thoroughly. He, however, appears to prescribe a greater variety of heights and projections to pedestals than any other author. He divides the pedestals into three sorts, according to the magnitude of the edifices in which they are to be employed, and makes their height, if I understand him rightly, to consist of from one-quarter to six times the height of the base, and their projections as far as one-third of their own respective heights. But such a loose manner of prescribing rules for the dimensions of architectural members must be considered objectionable, and but little compatible with science and taste.

In a Tamil fragment of a manuscript, purporting to be a translation of *Mayamata,* it is said—"The height of the shaft or pillar is to be divided into four parts. and one to be given to the base, which may or may not be accompanied by a pedestal; and in the case where a pedestal is joined to the base, the height of the pedestal may be either equal to that of the base, or twice or three times as much." Here, the greatest height given to a pedestal, namely, 'three times' that of the base, is equal to a little more than a third part of the highest column, which is not perhaps a bad proportion.

According to *Manasara,* there are three kinds of pedestals; of which the first is called *vedibhadra,* the second *pratibhadra,* and the third *manchabhadra.* Each of these are again divided into four sorts, making in all twelve, and each differing from the other in formation and in its ornaments, whatever may be its height in regard to the base with which it is connected. The remainder of this chapter is taken up with a detailed enumeration of the parts composing the different sorts of pedestals, but as I have marked the proportions in the designs themselves (Plate I), it would be superfluous to specify them in this place. To enable the reader, however, to form a judgement on the original rules from which the drawings are made, the following extracts respecting the three principal kinds of pedestals are submitted.

"The height of the *upapitha* (pedestal) being divided into twenty-four parts, let five be given to the *upana,*[1] one to the *campa,*[2] twelve to the *cantha,*[3] one to the *campa* again, four to the *pattica,*[4] and one to the *campa* above." This refers to the first sort of pedestal of the kind called *vedibhadra* (Fig. 1).

"Divide the height of the *upapuha* into twenty-six parts, and let three be given to the *upana,* one to the *campa,* two to the *padma,*[5] one to the *campa,* eleven to the *cantha,* one to the *campa,* two to the *padma,*[6] three to the *capota,* one to the *alinga,* and one to the *antarita,"* This refers to the first sort of the pedestal called *pratibhadra* (Fig. 5).

"Let the height of the *upapitha* be divided into thirty equal parts, give three to the *upana,* a half to the *campa,* three to the *mahambuja,* a half to the *campa,* two to the *candhara,* a half to the *campa,* a half to the *cshudra-padma,* two and a half to the *capota,* two to the *prativajina,* eight to the *gala,* one to the *uttira,* a half to the *campa,* a half to the *padma,* three to the upper *capota,* and two and a half to the *alinga,"* etc. This refers to the first sort of the pedestal called *manchabhadra* (Fig. 9).

This chapter closes with rules respecting the projection of the highest and of the most prominent parts of the pedestal, etc. in these words:

> The projection of the base or *upana* is equal to its height, or two, three, or four times as much more than its height; that of the *padma* is also equal to or twice as much as its height; and that of the *cumuda* or the *capota* is always equal to, or something less than its own height. The *padma* should be ornamented with the petals of the lotus, the square fillets with forms of gems, blossoms, foliages, etc., and the *cantha* with figures of *vyalas,*[7] *sinhas,*[8] or of leaves, flowers, and the like.

---

1. Plinth.
2. Fillet.
3. Dado.
4. Platland.
5. Cima reversa.
6. Cima recta.
7. A fabulous animal.
8. Lion.

OF BASES

The height of a base is equal to either a half, three-quarters, or a whole diameter of the shaft. When placed under pillars of an inferior sort, in porticoes and the like, and without a pedestal, its height is stated to be one-fourth, or one-third of that of the whole pillar. To bases, or rather basements, raised under pilasters in *vimanas,* etc., *Manasara* gives twelve different heights, to be used in so many different storeys one above another; the first height consisting of thirty *angulas,* and the last of four *hastas,* each of the intermediate ones being increased in the proportion of six *angulas*. The same author also prescribes the heights of pedestals to be constructed in the houses of the several classes, as follows: Brahmans should have them of four *hastas;* Cshetriyas, of three; Vaisyas, of two; and Sudras, of one *hasta*. The remaining parts of this chapter enumerate, at much length, the proportions of the component parts of no less than sixty-four different sorts of bases, under various denominations, as *pratibandha, ecabandha, prati-crama pushpepusbcala, sribandha, manchabandha, srenibandha,* etc.; but as it would be extremely tedious to repeat in detail the measures of the different members of each sort, I pass them over here, referring the reader to Plates II and III, which contain designs of twenty-eight sorts of bases, with the heights and projections of all their parts therein notified.

OF PILLARS

The fifteenth chapter of the *Manasara* treats of the several sorts of pillars, their various dimensions, forms, and ornaments, as does likewise the ninth section of the *Casyapa*: the two together seem to afford all the requisite information on this head. "The height of a pillar," says *Manasara,* "when placed on a base only, or both on a base and pedestal, is measured from the plinth (of the former) up to the lowest part of the entablature," that is, from the base to the capital inclusive. A passage in the *Casyapa* states that the measurement may also be taken from the cimbia of the shaft, exclusive of the base. "Let the height of the pillar," continues the first-mentioned author, "be divided into twelve, eleven, ten, nine, or eight parts, and one be taken for the breadth of the foot of the shaft; and the same being divided again by the number of parts of which the height of the pillar may consist, let the upper extremity of it be diminished by one of those parts respectively." "The height of the pillar," states the *Casyapa,* "may be three times that of the base, or six or eight times that of the pedestal; the breadth of the pillar may be a sixth, seventh, eighth, ninth, or tenth part of its height; if it be made of wood or stone, one-third, or one-fourth, or one-sixth of the height if it be a pilaster joined to a wall, (*cudyastambha*)."

Various names are given to pillars, by way of distinction, with regard to their forms: "A square pillar is called *brahmacanta*; an octangular one, *vishnucanta*; that which is circular or has sixteen sides, *rudracanta*; that which has five sides, *sivacanta*; and that which has six sides, *schandacanta*." The whole shaft may be of the same form, or in pillars of other forms, than square; the bottom, middle, and top may be quadrangular, and the intermediate spaces of other forms. "If the whole shaft from bottom to top be uniformly cylindrical and devoid of ornament, it is called *chandracanta*."

A minute technical description is given here by the two authors above-mentioned, of the various ornaments with which the several sorts of pillars are adorned, but as an accurate idea can be formed of them only by ocular observation of these decorations, it has been deemed unnecessary to follow our text too closely on this subject. It may, however, be useful to take a general view of the different kinds of pillars and their ornaments as described by *Manasara,* illustrating them by designs, partly taken from his descriptions, and partly from the models found in temples and porticoes of a pure Hindu style.

Pillars of Indian architecture may, with respect to the dimensions, be divided into seven sorts.

The first sort[1] is a column six diameters high; it is rarely made but upon a high base and pedestal. The entablature is more than half the altitude of the column; and the intercolumniation generally four diameters. The pedestal is of the second sort of the *pratibandha* kind (see Plate I); and its height is equal to that of the base, which is one-third of that of the column itself, or two diameters. The base is called *manchabandha,* and is divisible into thirty parts. The capital is equal in height to the upper diameter of the shaft, and its projection is equal to its height. The form of the capital is called *pushpabandha.* "The height of the capital," says *Manasara,* "may be either equal to the breadth of the shaft, or one-half or three-quarters of it, according as it may appear proportionate to the size of the column." Let the breadth of it be either one, one-and-a-quarter, half, or three-quarters of the diameter." I cannot find in any of the authors a description of this capital, and it is only mentioned by name by *Manasara* and others. I have given the design of it from the specimens found in buildings in the vicinity of Madras; and the artists call it in Tamil *putaleibodicai,* literally "flower-headed capital."

The entablature placed on this column does not differ from that placed on other pillars, except, perhaps, in the height, which I have already stated to be very great. On this subject *Manasara* observes generally, "The whole height of the entablature may be either three-quarters, one, one-and-a-quarter, one-and-a-half, one-and-three-quarters, or twice that of the base." "The height of the entablature may be a half, one-fourth, or three-quarters of that of the shaft." "Or the height of the pillar being divided into eight parts, six, five, three, or two may be given to that of the entablature." "The height of the entablature is measured from the architrave up to the corona." Its form will be described in another place."

The second sort of column is seven diameters in height; it is placed in most examples upon a base and pedestal; the base is two diameters high; it belongs to the species called *cumbhandha* (See Plate II).

The pedestal is equal in height to three-fourths of the base, and is of the kind called *vedibhadra* (Plate I). The column is also placed, as may be seen in another design (Plate IV), only on a pedestal, which is equal to half the height of the pillar, and which is one of the sorts called *munchabhadra.* The capital given to the first design of this pillar is taken from a model found at *Tiruvattur,* near Madras; it is the same which *Manasara* and others

1. In the following description of pillars, every member belonging to an order is considered, and particularly the entablature, which is made the subject of a distinct chapter in the *Manasara.*

call *tarangabodhica,* and is one diameter high and projects equal to its height. Speaking of this sort of capital, *Manasara* says, "it should be decorated with *tarangas*[1] and other appropriate ornaments; the height of the capital being divided into twelve parts, let the form of *tarangas* occupy three of them, let the *bodhica* (capital), which should resemble the cobra de capello, occupy six, and adorned with flowers and the like, and let one part above this be given to * * *,[2] one to the *cima,* and one to the *listel*. The projecting part of the *bodhica* should be fashioned like the stalk of a plantain flower. At the upper extremity are the *tarangas,* of equal height or something more. The lower part of the head of the *bodhica* is one-third of the upper in breadth, and a third of the former being divided into five parts, one of them is given to the cavetto, one to the fillet, two to the *cima,* and one to the *listel*: and the whole should be decorated with foliages, rows of gems, and the like." In another place the same author says, "Let the capital *(bodhica)* be made to consist of one, two, three, four, five, or six faces, according to the situation in which it is placed."

The other form of capital given to the column in the second design is taken from a *mantapa* at Maylapur. It is to be met with in many other ancient buildings, and is what the artists call in Tamil *surul-bodhica,* roll capital. I cannot find any particular description of it, except a passage in the *Manasara,* which says, "the projecting ornaments on the sides of the capital are made either in the form of an inverted apex or of a *chacra,* wheel, or circle." It is one diameter in height, and projects but three-quarters of the diameter.

There is not any particular rule respecting the intercolumniation of these or any other sorts of pillars; but in porticoes, where these pillars are found, the space between one column and another exceeds three diameters. The general rule laid down in the *Manasara* is this: "The intercolumniation may be either two, three, four, or five diameters; it is measured in three ways, first from the inner extremity of the base of one pillar to that of another; secondly. from the centre of the two pillars; and, thirdly, from the outer extremities of the pillars including the two bases." The latter method of measuring the intercolumniations is, I am inclined to believe, applicable to the pilasters in gateways or temples only, not to simple colonnades.

The third sort of column, with its base and capital, is eight diameters high, with a diminution of the shaft at the top of the eighth part of the thickness at its bottom. The base occupies half a diameter, and this height is to be divided into ten parts; two to be given to the plinth, one to the fillet; three to the *cimacia* and its fillet, one and a half to the cavetto, the same to the torus, and one to the *cimbia*. The whole projection of the base is half of its height. The following passage from the *Manasara* refers to this kind of base: "Let a base ornamented with the lotus be made under the foot of the pillar, one or two diameters in height, and let it be adorned with figures of demons, lions, and the like."

The height of the capital, which is made after the manner of the *phalaca,*[3] is three-quarters of the lower diameter of the column, and is divided into thirteen parts; two are

1. Literally waves, a term applied to denote the projecting moulding employed in capitals, terminating by a number of undulating lines. See Plate IV. fig. 2.
2. Here, a word in the original manuscript is not legible.
3. The forms of this ornament may be seen in Plate VI.

given to the abacus, one to the fillet, two to the *madana*,[1] seven to the cimarecta, and one to the cimbia. The upper part of the shaft, about one-and-a-half diameters below the capital, being divided into twenty-four parts, three are given to the collarino with its fillet, three to the ovolo, three to the lower collarino, five to the lower torus with its cimacia, and ten below to the strings of pearls (*muctadhama*).[1] The projection of the capital is one diameter, or about an eighth part beyond that of the lowest part of the base; the fillets project the full, and the torus three-quarters of their respective heights.

The height of the entablature is one-fourth of that of the column. It is to be divided into twenty-one parts, eight are given to the architrave, seven to the cornice, and six to the *vyalam*.[2] Of the eight parts of the architrave, one is to be given to the cavetto, three to the tema or benda (*uttara*) with its listels, two to the cimarecta, and two to the upper facia (*vajina*). Of the seven parts of the cornice, one occupies the fillet, and the remainder the ovolo (*prastara*); and of the six parts of the cornice, three to be given to the cavetto, two to the *prativajina,* and one to the fillet. The projection of the *vajina*[3] of the architrave is equal to that of the capital, that of the *prastara* is twice as much, and that of the cornice equal to its own height. After making a similar division of the entablature, our author lays down the following rule respecting the projection of the members. "The height of the architrave being divided into four, five, six, seven, or eight parts, one should be given to its projection beyond the pillars. The *capota*[4] projects equal to its height, or to three-fourths of it, and the *vajina* one-fourth." "The *alinga* recedes about one diameter, and the *antarita* projects equal to its own height, and the same may be said of the *prati.*"

The fourth sort of column is nine diameters high. The base is one of those called *pratibhadra,* and is one diameter in height. It is without a pedestal.

The base is to be divided into eighteen equal parts, two to be given to the plinth, one to its fillet, three to the cimarecta, three to the cavetto with its listel, three to the torus, three to the upper cavetto, two to the platband, and one to the cimbra. The projection of the plinth is one-third of the height of the whole base; the torus and the platband project equal to their respective heights.

The upper ornaments of this column occupy two diameters, and the capital takes three-quarters of the diameter, which is to be divided into ten parts: two to be given to the abacus, which projects half a diameter, one to the strings of pearls, one to the fillet, four to the cimacia, and one to the circular cimbia. The ornaments under the capital are to be divided into sixteen parts: of which give two to the cavetto or collarino, one-and-a-half to the cima, four to the torus, which projects perpendicular to the plinth, or three-quarters part of its height; one-and-a-half to the lower cima, three to the lower collarino, two to the astragal, which projects equal to its own height, and two to the third cima and its fillet, below which a space equal to three diameters is taken up by strings of pearls, but which are omitted in some columns of a similar description.

---

1. The forms of this ornament may be seen in Plate VI.
2. A moulding used above the cornice, and which takes its name from being generally ornamented with the figures of the animal called *vyala*.
3. A square moulding so called.
4. The projecting member of the cornice.

The fifth sort of column is ten diameters high, including the base, which ought to be three-quarters of the diameter. It should be divided into twelve parts: two for the plinth, whose projection is a fourth part of the diameter, one for the fillet, four for the cima, and one-and-a-half for the cavetto, one for the lesser cima, one-and-a-half for the torus, and one for the cimbia. The projection of the cima and torus is equal to their respective heights. This column is sometimes erected on a high pedestal, which is about a third part of the height of the pillar.

The height of the capital, which is called *pushpabandha,* is equal to the upper diameter of the column: its projection on the sides is equal to its height, and the middlemost square is ornamented with the petals of a lotus. "The altitude of the capital," says Casyapa, "may be equal to the higher, lower, or the middle diameter of the column. Its breadth may be equal to its height, or four or five diameters." "A capital the height of which is from one to two diameters, and the breadth twice its height, is of the superior sort; and that which in height is half the diameter, and in breadth from one to three diameters, is of the inferior sort."

In colonnades of porticoes, the intercolumniations are found to be from one diameter and a half to two diameters.

The sixth sort of pillar is eleven diameters high. The design made to illustrate this is selected from among the pillars found at Canjeveram; it represents a square pillar of the same height, exclusive of the base, which is composed of a plinth, a cimarecta, and torus, with their fillets, and is one diameter high. The same pillar, including the base, may be taken as an example also of the seventh sort, which ought to be twelve diameters in height.[1] "When the pillar," says Casyapa, "is measured in height from the upper fillet of the base it is called *nigata-stambha,* but when it is measured from the plinth below it, is termed *nichata-stambha.*"

At the foot of the shaft, a space equal in height to the hypothenuse of the lower diameter is made quadrangular, around which are sculptured images of the deities, and the like, in bas-relief. In about half a diameter above this, is made the ornament called *nagabandha.*[2] The remainder of the shaft, about three diameters and a half, is made to consist of eight sides, including the strings of pearls, which occupy three-quarters of a diameter, and appear to be suspended from the fillet of the upper ornament called *padmabandha,*[3] which takes up half a diameter. Next above this is the *calasa* or water-pot, about three-quarters of a diameter; and above this are made, with the same height given to them, three other mouldings, called in the language of architecture, *herica, asya,* and *tatica,* which last projects a fourth part of the diameter. Above these again is the lower collarino, in height about a quarter of a diameter, then the ornament called *cumbha,* which is half a diameter high and projects as much; next the upper collarino, a little less than the lower one; next the moulding called *phalaca,* which is one diameter high, and projects equal to its height; next the third collarino, about three-fourths of a diameter;

1. See Plate VI.
2. A sort of moulding made in the form of a serpent.
3. A moulding made in the form of a lotus.

and last of all, the capital of the kind called *pushpabandha,* which has already been described.[1]

This pillar may, according to the definition of its form, be called *vishnucanta,* and appears in most of its ornaments, though not in their proportions, to agree with the description given by *Manasara* of that which he called *palicastambha.* He says,

> the height of the collarino *(viracantha)* should be one diameter of the column; that of the *phalaca,* one, three-quarters, or two or three diameters, and its projection one-fourth of its height. The height of the *cumbha* below the collarino may be half, one-and-a-half, or two diameters, and its breadth equal to the upper or lower collarino. The height of the *taticasya*[2] is half, or three-quarters of the diameter. Let the lower cima be equal to its height, and let its breadth be one-and-a-quarter diameter. Below that comes the *herica* of half that height. The height and breadth of the *tatica* are equally one diameter. Below that let a *calasa* (water-pot) be made about two diameters in breadth, and let the upper part of it be shaped in the form of a *durdhura* flower, and in such a manner as may appear graceful. Below this, about three-quarters of the diameter should be decorated with strings of pearls.

Besides the model referred to in the above description, Plate XVI contains three more designs of pillars, which may also serve as specimens of those of the seventh sort, so far at least as their dimensions are concerned. The pillars which they represent are to be seen in a portico at *Tiruvanamalei,* but I cannot find anything in the description of pillars contained in the books under examination, like the works sculptured on the shafts of these models. They are probably modern improvements, and their workmanship, like that which adorns the pillars at *Madura,* may be attributed to the skill of the artists of the day. The same may be said of the double pillars which support a beautiful portico at Canjeveram, "and on which are sculptured, in alto relief, lions and horses standing upright the full length of the columns; the former treading on elephants, and the latter mounted by armed knights" (See Plates XVII and XVIII).

The pillars at Tiruvanamalei are estimated to be about thirty feet high, with proportionate thickness, diminished at the top by a twelfth part of the lower diameter. There are three kinds of them. The first is placed on a high pedestal and base: the whole shaft is divided into ten compartments, each being equal in height to the hypothenuse of the diameter of the pillar; and on all the four sides of these compartments are sculptured, in relief, four small pillars or pilasters supporting an entablature. The second pillar differs from the first in having two, instead of four, small ornamental pilasters in relief, on each side of the ten compartments into which the shaft is divided, with an ornamented niche in the middle, which in the third specimen is flanked by two small *panjaras* or ornamented cages on both sides of it. The second sort of pillar is placed on a base without a pedestal, and the third on a pedestal without a base (See Plate XVI).

Having taken the preceding general survey of the several members connected with the orders of Indian architecture, it was my intention to submit a few remarks on such of the orders now in use in modern Europe, as have any correspondence with those of

1. See page 30, and Plate VI.
2. See Plate VI.

India; but being destitute of European books which treat directly on this subject, I confine myself to the Egyptian, Grecian, and Roman, and to them only with regard to a few leading particulars.

The difference in the Indian orders consists chiefly in the proportion between the thickness and height of pillars; while that of the Grecian and Roman orders depends not only on the dimensions of columns, but also on the form of the other parts belonging to them.

Concerning the proportions of columns, the second sort of column in the Hindu architecture may be compared with the Tuscan, the third with the Doric, the fourth with the Ionic, and the fifth with the Corinthian or Composite pillar. This affinity between the columns of India and of Rome and Greece is so striking that one would be apt to ascribe it to something more than mere chance, but there are other columns in the Indian architecture, not only one diameter lower than the Tuscan, but from one to two diameters higher than the Composite.

The Egyptian columns appear to have no fixed proportion in regard to thickness and height. In some of the specimens of the ruins of Upper Egypt, the height of the columns consists of from four to six times the lower diameter, which last proportion coincides with that of the first sort of the Indian pillar.

The orders of India, and of Greece and Rome, are remarkable for the beautiful effect of their proportions, a circumstance to which little regard has been paid by the Egyptians.

Both the Indian and Grecian columns are diminished gradually in their diameter from the base to the summit of the shaft, a practice which has never been observed in the Egyptian; on the contrary, a diametrically opposite rule has been observed in their shafts, which are made narrower at the bottom than at the top, and placed upon a square or round plinth.

The proportion in which the diminution at the top of the columns of the two former is made, seems to have been regulated by the same principle, though not by the same rule. The general rule adopted by the Hindu architects in this respect is that the thickness at the bottom, being divided into as many parts as there are diameters in the whole height of the column, one of these parts is invariably diminished at the top; but in the Grecian and Roman architecture, the diameter of the upper part of the shaft, in a column of fifteen feet in height, is made one-sixth less than its thickness at the base; and in a column' of fifty feet, the diminution is one-eighth. The higher the columns are, the less they diminish, because, the apparent diminution of the diameter in columns of the same proportion is always greater according to their height, and this principle is supposed to have been discovered with great scientific skill, and is adduced as one of the proofs of the highly refined taste of the Greeks; but we observe that precepts derived from the same principle have been taught and practised in India from time immemorial.

The plan of the Grecian and Roman columns is always round; but the plan of the Hindu columns admits of every shape, and is frequently found in the quadrangular and octangular form, and richly adorned with sculptured ornaments. The form of the Egyptian pillars, too, is circular, and their shafts are often fluted like the Corinthian, but the fluting of the Indian columns resembles neither the one nor the other. The decorations of the

Egyptian columns often consist in representations "of a bundle of reeds" tied up with a cord on the top, having a square stone placed over it; in some specimens are also found bindings or fillets in various parts of the shaft, and in the interval between them, reeds and hieroglyphics are represented. But there is nothing like these ornaments in the Indian orders, except in the columns found in the excavated temple of Elephanta, and some other places, and which differ materially from those employed in other situations in Hindustan.

There are no fixed intercolumniations in the Hindu architecture, as are found in the Grecian, but the spaces allowed between pillar and pillar in different Hindu buildings, are found nearly to coincide with the Grecian mode of intercolumniations, though in too many instances they differ widely from it, and the same may perhaps be said of the Egyptian colonnades.

The Indian pedestals and bases are made more systematically, and afford by far a greater variety of proportions and ornaments, than the Grecian and Roman. In the European architecture, the forms and dimensions of the pedestals and bases are fixed by invariable rules, with respect to the orders in which they are employed; but in the Indian, the choice is left to the option of the artists.

The capitals of the Grecian columns invariably mark the distinction of the several orders: those of the Indian are varied at pleasure, though not without regard to the diameter and length of the shaft; and the forms of the plainest of them, though they have in reality nothing in common with the Grecian order, are found at a distant view to hear some resemblance to the Doric and Ionic capitals; but those of a more elaborate kind are sometimes so overloaded with a sort of filligree ornaments, as to destroy the effect of the beautiful proportions of the whole. The Egyptian capitals, on the other hand, are formed into elegant vase shapes, decorated with the stalks, leaves, and blossoms of the lotus, and occasionally with palm leaves, which latter ornaments are supposed to have given the first idea of the Corinthian capitals. And in some specimens, the Egyptian capital is composed of the representation of the head of the goddess Isis.

The entablature of the Indian order admits of little variety, as well in its composition, as in its relative proportions, whereas the same member in the Grecian and Roman architecture is varied for each order both in form and magnitude. The massiveness of the Indian entablature offers a striking contrast to the lightness of the Grecian; but the richness of the former may be said to be unrivalled.

In the existing treatises on Hindu architecture, no mention is made of anything like a substitution of human figures for columns to support the entablature, but the shaft is directed to be adorned with the figures of demons and animals; yet various examples are to be met with in which human figures, as well as representations of animals, are employed in bold relief in the sides of pillars in temples and porticoes, but by no means like those found in Egyptian architecture. The antiquity of this invention in India is not determined, but the Grecian architects refer the origin of their caryatides to the commemoration of their captivity of the Caryan women, while others assert that it was derived from an Egyptian source.

We now return to the ninth chapter of the *Manasara,* which treats of villages and towns, and this being made to appear as belonging to architecture, inasmuch as it regards the formation of streets and the allotment of suitable sites for the building of temples, piazzas, etc., I beg leave to subjoin a few extracts from it, trusting that the rules which they contain will serve to trace out the principles upon which a Hindu village or town is built, and that they will not be altogether uninteresting to those who delight in Indian antiquities.

> The extent of villages or towns is declared to admit of forty varieties, consisting of from five hundred to twenty thousand *dandas* square, each sort exceeding the one immediately below it by five hundred *dandas*. The whole area of a village, with the lands thereunto belonging, being divided into twenty equal parts, one is assigned for the occupation of Brahmans, six or more for that of the three other classes, and the remainder for agriculture.
>
> A street that goes round the village or town is called *mangalavithi,* which should be from one to five *dandas* in width. That which runs from east to west is called *rajapatha*; that which has gates on both sides, *rajavithi;* that which has *sandhis* or angles, *sandhivithi*; and that which is in a southerly direction, *mahacala* or *vamana*.
>
> Previously to building villages, towns, etc., let the *sthapati* trace upon the ground selected for the purpose, any of the mystical figures described in the seventh chapter, and particularly that which is called *paramasayica,*[1] and after offering the prescribed sacrifices to the deities presiding over its various parts, let him proceed to arrange the streets, and mark out sites for building temples, etc., according to the rules laid down in the *Sastras*.
>
> There are eight sorts of villages or towns, namely, 1. *dandaca* (that which resembles a staff); 2. *sarvatobhadra* (in every respect happy); 3. *nandyavartta* (the abode of happiness); 4. *padmaca* (that which has the form of a lotus flower); 5. *swastica* (that which resembles the mystical figure so named); 6. *prastara* (that which has the shape of a conch); 7. *carmuca* (that which resembles a bow); and 8. *chaturmucha* (that which has four faoes).
>
> The village called *dandaca* is quadrangular, and surrounded by a square wall. It consists of from one to five parallel streets, running in one direction, generally from east to west, and of two more streets forming right angles at both the extremities of the five parallel streets, and also of a third crossing the middle of them. The breadth of the streets is from one to five *dandas,* and the middlemost may be made broader than the rest. The streets at the extremities or near the walls have a single row of houses; the centre streets a double row, or one on each side. The space occupied by each house should be from three to five *dandas* broad, and from two to four *dandas* long. There should be four large gates, one on each side of the enclosing wall of the village, and as many smaller ones at the several angles. In the part presided over by *Varuna* or *Maytra,* should be erected a temple for Vishnu; and in that presided over by

1. The seventh chapter of the *Manasara* describes certain mystical figures which are traced on the ground plan of villages, etc. for the purpose not only of offering oblations and sacrifices to the divinities who are supposed to preside over their various parts, but also of dividing the area into several compartments, to be applied, according to their supposed fitness, to the building of temples, and the formation of high roads, streets, etc.; to each of which purposes the part over which a certain deity presides is considered more adapted than any other. An enumeration of the several figures, and of the deities presiding over their various parts, would however be little interesting or instructive to the European reader.

Adita, at the north-east angle, one dedicated to Siva; a shrine, for Chamunda,[1] should be built near the north gate without the wall. There should be two tanks[2] or reservoirs, one towards the south-west and the other towards the north-east. This village is particularly intended for the residence of Brahmans. It may contain twelve, twenty-four, fifty, one hundred and eight, three hundred or more houses. The smallest, or that which contains twelve houses, is called *asrama,* hermitage, and ought to be situated near mountains and forests, for the habitation of hermits. The village containing twenty-four houses is to be situated on the banks of a river, and inhabited by *yatis* or holy mendicants: it is called *puram.* That which contains fifty houses should be occupied by those who have performed holy sacrifices, or by householders in general: in the former case, it is called *puram,* and in the latter *mangalam.* The village containing a hundred and eight houses is commonly called *Costham.*

The village called *Sarvatobhadra* is also of a quadrangular form, containing in the middle a temple dedicated, to any one of the triad, Brahma,[3] Vishnu, or Maheswara. It has four streets of equal length on the four sides within the wall, meeting one another at right angles, and two more crossing each other in the middle. Between these may be formed three, four, five, or as many more streets as the extent of the village will admit on each side parallel to the middlemost street.

Here several verses in the original bear allusion to the projections of some of the streets described above, but they are not sufficiently clear to be translated.

"Without the walls," continues our text,

should be placed the shrines of the deities who preside over and defend the several quarters of the village; at the angular points should be erected halls, porticos, colleges, and other public edifices; and towards the quarter of *agni* (south-east), a water-shed for the accommodation of travellers and passengers. The whole village should be secured by a quadrangular wall, and a ditch around it, with four large and as many small gates, in the middle of the sides and at the angular points. Without the northern gate should be erected a temple for the worship of Maha Cali, and the huts of the *chandalas* or outcasts should be a *crosa*[4] distant from the village. A tank or reservoir should be constructed either on the south or north side, or near either of these two points, for ablutionary and culinary purposes.

The village called *Nandyavartta* is either square or oblong. It is divisible into as many parts as are contained in the (mystic) figure called *Chandita* or *Paramasayica.* The *Chandita* contains sixty-four equal parts, being the square of eight, of which the middle four parts are called *Brahmya,* or those which belong to Brahma, and they should be entirely appropriated to sacred purposes. Around these are twelve parts called *Divya,* or those belonging to the Devas; around these twenty parts called *Manushya,* or those belonging to mortals; and

1. The goddess of destruction, a form of *Bhavani.*
2. The south of India is famous for the beautiful workmanship of its reservoirs, which are generally very spacious, and completely lined with stone, furnished with steps, and ornamented with pavilions, etc.
3. The worship of the representation of Brahma is very rare.
4. A *crosa* is equal to four thousand yards.

> around these again twenty-eight called *Paysacha,* or those belonging to demons. These several rounds should be occupied by different classes in the order of their superiority, that is Brahmans[1] should have the *Brahmya,* and so with the rest. The figure called *Paramasayica* contains eighty-one equal parts, being the square of nine, of which the middle nine are *Brahmya;* sixteen around these are *Divya;* twenty-four around these *Manushya,* and the outermost thirty-two *Paysacha.* This village has four large streets along the inside of the wall by which it is surrounded, running in each direction at right angles; namely, one near the north-west quarter, passing towards the north-east, projects at a small distance beyond the cross street, which intersects it; another opening from a little way within the projection runs forward in a south-east direction, and projects in the same manner beyond the intersecting street on that side, and the same may be said of the streets at the two other angular points. The number of streets in the outer compartment should be determined according to its extent, and in the compartments called *Divya* aud *Manushya,* three or four more parallel streets may be made from east to west, with as many cross ones from north to south, forming as it were so many courts or enclosures. Two broad streets run through the middle of the village, from east to west and from north to south, cutting one another in the middle, where there should be erected either a temple for Brahma, or a *mantapa* for general meetings. At each of the angles of the outermost streets there should be a gateway ornamented with arches and the like. This village is of two sorts, which are also called the one *Mangalam* and the other *Puram.* The former is inhabited only by Brahmans, and the latter by all classes indiscriminately.

In this manner, the author goes on to describe the forms and arrangements of the remaining sorts of villages; but as the accompanying designs (Plates XLIII to XLVI) will, it is hoped, render the subject more intelligible, I shall close this article with one or two more extracts only, respecting the sites and aspects of temples, and regarding some other matters treated of in this chapter.

> The temples of Vishnu, in whatever form that deity may be worshipped, should be erected within the village facing towards the east, except in the incarnation of Narasinha (the Man-lion), whose temple should be built without the wall with its face turned from the village or town. That part of the figure which belongs to *Mitra,*[2] *Bhallata,*[2] *Arya,*[2] or *Sauruya,*[2] should be invariably assigned to the temple of Vishnu, but the shrine of Siva should be built in the compartments presided over by Indra,[2] Indraja,[2] Rudra,[2] Rudraga,[2] etc. If the emblem of Siva (*Linga*) is to be consecrated according to the *Siddhanta Agama,*[3] it may be placed within the village; if otherwise, it should remain without. In the case of Vishnu too,

---

1. This is a contradiction of the preceding passage, which directs the middle parts called *Brahmya* to be appropriated to religious structures.
2. Denoting certain compartments in the mystic figure before mentioned.
3. The title of a religious book held in high reverence by the followers of Siva, and which treats, first of several species of charities, such as the building of a caravanserai, and digging of tanks and wells for the accommodation of travellers; secondly, of religious duties diurnal and periodical, of the various kinds of sacraments, and of ceremonies propitious or expiative, in which which are included the holy incantations wherewith temples are sanctified, and images of deities deified and adorned; and lastly, of the nature of the godhead and his attributes, of souls, elements, and other principles, and of contemplation, etc.

if the idol is to be consecrated according to the system of *Vaikhanasa*,[1] it may be admitted within, but if according to the doctrines of *Pancharatra*[2] it should be placed without the village. The shrines of Durga, Shanmucha,[3] and the objects worshipped by Jainas and Bauddhas, should be erected without the village.

Private houses or mansions may consist of from one to nine storeys, but this is to be determined according to the rank of the persons for whom they are built. The lower classes of people must on no account construct their houses of more than a single storey or ground floor; and the height of the buildings should correspond in every street, as far as practicable, and in all structures of the same number of storeys.

The front, middle, and back-door of a private dwelling-house should be so contrived as to be on the same level, and in the same straight line one with another. Let the outer door be placed, not exactly in the middle of the façade, but a little more to one side than to the other. The general practice is this: if the front of the house be ten paces in length, the entrance should be between five on the right and four on the left. The same rule is to be observed with regard to the gates of temples. In the front of the houses should be erected a *vedica*, or raised seat or pedestal on each side of the door.

The gates and doorways of temples and houses of all classes of people should be from one *hasta*[3] and a half to seven *hastas* in height; the smaller doors, from one to five *hastas*; and the windows, from twelve *angulas* to one *hasta* and a half. The breadth of large gates should be equal to, or a little less than, half of their height; or, the height of the door being divided into nine parts, five may be given to its breadth. The height of the door-frame being divided into seven, eight, nine, or ten equal parts, that of the void space should be equal to that of the door-frame, minus one part; a strict conformity to these rules will insure prosperity and happiness.

A whole page after this is employed in enumerating the various sorts of gifts and donations to be made to the artists on the completion of an edifice, and finally in denouncing dire misfortunes to those who withhold such presents from them.

The next chapter professes to describe *nagaras* or cities; but as it contains nothing farther than an enumeration of several sorts of cities and the various titles of particular princes who are qualified to reside in them, I shall omit it altogether. In order, however, that some idea may be formed of an ancient Hindu city, I subjoin the following extract from the first book of the *Ramayana*.

On the banks of the Sarayu is a vast, fertile, and delightful country called Cosala, abounding in corn and wealth.

In that country is a city called Ayodhya, greatly famed in this world, and built by *Manu* himself, the lord of men. This great and prosperous city was twelve *yojanas*[4] in length and three in breadth, and stored with all conveniences. The streets and lanes were admirably disposed, and the high-roads were well sprinkled with water. In this city lived Dasaratha,

1. Two rival systems of religious rites and prayers observed among the followers of Vishnu.
2. The wife of Siva, an avenging goddess, and her son Carticeya.
3. This perhaps alludes to the height of a window, which follows.
4. A *yojana* is equal to nine miles.

the most potent of monarchs, even as Indra lived in Amaravati.[1] It is adorned with arched gateways and beautiful ranges of shops; it is fortified with numerous defences and warlike machines, and inhabited by all sorts of skilful artists. It was crowded with bards and musicians, filled with riches, and shone forth with unrivalled glory; it had lofty towers stored with fire-arms and adorned with banners. It was constantly filled with female stage players; it was beautiful with gardens and groves of mango-trees, and enclosed with high walls. It was surrounded by impassable ditches, and secured by fortifications difficult of assault by foreign kings; it was full of horses, elephants, cattle, camels, and mules. It was ornamented with palaces of exquisite workmanship, lofty as mountains, and enriched with jewels, abounding with beautiful houses consisting of several storeys, and it shone like Indrás heaven. It was crowded with tributary princes, purified with sacrificial rites, and filled with merchants of foreign countries. Its aspect had an enchanting effect; and the whole city was diversified with various colours, and decorated with regular avenues of sweet-scented trees. It was full of precious stones, and resplendent with stately edifices and beautiful apartments. It was filled with buildings erected close to one another, and without intermediate voids, and situated on a smooth level ground. It abounded in delicious rice, and water sweet as the juice of sugarcane. It incessantly echoed with the sounds of kettle-drums, tabors, cymbals, and lutes; this city truly surpassed any that was ever beheld on earth. The houses which it contained resembled the celestial mansions which the *Siddhas* obtain through the virtue of their austerity.

Of the remaining portion of the *Manasara,* twelve successive chapters, from the eighteenth to the twenty-ninth, are entirely taken up with rules respecting the measurements, etc. of as many sorts of *vimanas* or pyramidal temples. The same subject is also treated of in several sections of the *Casyapa.*

A *vimana* consists, according to the former, 'of from one to twelve storeys;' and according to the latter, 'of from one to sixteen storeys;' and 'is made round, quadrangular, or of six or eight sides.' The form of the edifice may be uniformly the same from the basement up to the spire, whether it be square, oblong, circular, oval, or the like; or it may be of a mixed nature, composed partly of one and partly of another form.'

A quadrangular temple is called *nagara,* an octaagular *dravidha,* and a circular *vesara.*

Vimanas are of three sorts, distinguished one from another by the principal materials of which they are formed, as *suddha,* pure; *misra,* mixed; and *sancirna,* anomalous. An edifice is called *suddha,* which is composed of but one kind of material, as stone, brick, etc., and this is considered the best of all. *Misra* is that which is composed of two kinds of materials, as brick and stone, or stone and metals; and *sancirna* is that which is composed of three or more kinds of materials, as timber, stone, brick, metal, etc.

Vimanas are further distinguished into three kinds, namely, *sthanaca, asana,* and *sayana;* the first having reference to the height, the second to the breadth, the third to the length. Moreover, the idol to be placed in the *vimana,* called *sthanaca,* should be in an erect posture; that to be placed in the *asana,* in a sitting; and that to be placed in the *sayana,* in a recumbent posture.

1. The capital of *Indra,* the regent of heaven.

Vimanas are again divided into five sorts, with respect to their magnitude. They are called *santica,*[1] *panstica,*[2] *jayada,*[3] *adbhuta,*[4] *sarvacama.*[5] The breadths of these five kinds of temples being divided into seven, six, five, four, and three parts in due order; ten, nine, eight, and seven of those parts are given to their respective heights.

Temples consist of the *garbhagriha* (the womb of the house), the *antarala* (the anti-temple), and the *ardha mantapa* (the front portico). The diameter of the whole length of the building, including the walls, is to be divided into four and a-half or six parts; and the *garbhagriha* to take up two, two and a half, or three; the *antarala,* one and a-half or two; and the *ardha mantapa,* one or one and a-half.[6]

Temples on a large scale have three or four successive porticoes attached to them in the front, which are called *ardha-mantapa, mahamantapa, sthapana mantapa, urittya mantapa,* etc. *Ardhamantapas* are sometimes made broader than the *garbhagriha,* in which case the width of the former is either one-and-a-half or twice that of the latter. In the event of the three compartments being of the same breadth, the length of the whole should be two-and-a-half the breadth.

The breadth of the *garbhagriha* being divided into three, four, five, seven, nine, eleven, thirteen, or fifteen parts, let two, three, four, five, six, seven, or eight be allowed to the interior space, and the remainder take up the thickness of the walls on all sides.

The thickness of the wall being divided into twelve equal parts, let five or six be given to the door-frames or posts without, and seven or eight to the inside of the door. The door-frames or posts maybe placed either in the middle or at the extremity of the point of the division before mentioned.

The height of the pillars of the *vimana* is to be divided into ten or eight equal parts; and nine, eight, or seven of them are given to that of the doorway, the breadth of which is to be half its height.

In temples, and houses of Brahmans and others, two-leafed doors may be used. The doors are turned either by means of a perpendicular cylinder, one end of which rests on the ground, or by hinges. The outside of the door-frames are ornamented with foliages, etc., and on the architrave of the door, and on both sides of it, are carved the images of the gods and goddesses presiding over gates and door-ways.

Let a water-spout be made over the base on the back wall of the *garbhagriha,* on the left side of the idol, either towards the east or the north, according as the temple may face towards

1. The moderate.
2. The bulky.
3. The victorious.
4. The admirable.
5. The universally beloved.
6. Sometimes a portico is made round the *garbhagriha* and *antarala* together, the whole being closed by walls on all the sides but the front, in which are the doors for entrance, approached by the front portico, which is generally a peristyle, and it serves as the innermost court around which people perform their circumambulations; I say the innermost court, because there are other courts around the whole temple.

> the south or the east. The thickness of the spout should be either eight, ten, twelve, fourteen, or sixteen *angulas*. Its length should be equal to the *adhisthana,* which length being divided into three equal parts, one is given to the projection below (*lambana*). The breadth of the bottom of the spout is to be divided into five parts, and three to be given to the breadth of the sloping extremity below. The whole spout being divided into five parts, three to be given to the *cudmala,*[1] one to the *padma,*[2] and one to the *vajina* or fillet. On the surface of the spout a cavity is to be made for discharging the water, from one to five *angulas* broad. The breadth of the cavity at the end should be three-fifths of that at the bottom. The spout, may be made to spring from the head of a lion, etc., and the whole so devised as to project like a plantain flower.

To these observations succeeds a detailed enumeration of the proportions of the different sorts of *vimanas,* consisting of from one to twelve storeys; but as it would be extremely tiresome to specify the whole, even in the most abridged form, I shall insert the measurements of a few sorts only, which, with the assistance of the designs that accompany this essay, will, it is hoped, serve as a standard by which to determine the proportions of the rest of this class of buildings.

A VIMANA CONSISTING OF A SINGLE STOREY
(See Plate XXI)

The breadth of this *vimana,* which is measured between the two angular pillars, is divided into six parts: two are given to the *muchbhadra* (or the middle niche), and two to the space on each side of it. The height of *vimanas* is measured from the base to the apex, exclusive of the pedestal below, and is equal to one-and-a-half of its breadth. Let the whole height be divided into eight equal parts; give one to the *adhisthana* (base), two to the *pada* (pillar), one to the *prastara* (entablature), one to the *griva* (the neck of the dome), two to the *sichara* (cupola), and one to the *sthupi* (pinnacle). The *adhisthana* (base) is divisible into twenty-six parts. The height of the *griva* being divided into three parts, one is given to the *vedhica* or basement, one to the *griva,*[3] and one to the *uttira* (entablature). The *sichara* (cupola) being divided into thirty-two parts, three are to be given to the *lupa mula,*[4] two to the *adhopadma* (the lower cima recta), one to the *malabaddha* (the fillet ornamented with a wreath), two to the *urddhvapadma* (the upper cima), sixteen to the *sichara* (dome), one to the *malabaddha,* two to the *chandrahnila,*[5] and five to the *mahapadma* (the great lotus). The breadth of the pavement being divided into six parts, one of which is diminished for the breadth of the *vedhica* (or base) on the first storey, which being divided into four parts, three of them are given to the breadth of the *griva*. The projection of the pendents is equal to the breadth of the *vedhica* below.

---

1. An ornament made in the form of a bud.
2. Lotus, or *cima recta*.
3. *Griva* is here used to signify that hollow space which supports an entablature under the cupola, though the term is generally applied to denote the whole ornament, consisting of the base, the hollow space, and the entablature before-mentioned.
4. A sloping and projecting member of the entablature, representing a continued pent roof. It is made below the cupola, and its ends are placed as it were suspended from the architrave, and reaching the stalk of the lotus below.
5. A horizontal moulding over the *sichara* and below the base of the pinnacle.

The breadth of the *sichara* being divided into five parts, three are to be given to that of the *pattica*,[1] which being divided into five parts, three-and-a-half are given to the breadth of the *padma* above, one-third of it to the *cumbha*, and one-third of the latter to the *cudmala* (the bud). Or, divide the crown of the cupola into five equal parts; give three to the breadth of the *phalaca*, which divide into five equal parts, make the breadth of the *padma* take up four parts; which divide again into three equal parts, give one to the breadth of the *cantha*, and three to the breadth of the *cumbha*. Divide the breadth of the latter into nine equal parts, and give one to that of the *danda* or pinnacle, or three times the breadth of the pinnacle may be taken for the breadth of the *phalaca*, and one-third of the breadth of the latter for that of the *cudmala* (bud).

The great *padma* or lotus under the pinnacle should be made to consist of eight petals, and the rest of the ornaments made in such a manner as to give a graceful appearance to the whole.

A VIMANA CONSISTING OF TWO STOREYS
(See Plate XXII)

The height is twice the breadth, which latter is divided into six parts; one to be given to the *carnacutha*,[2] one to the *harantara*,[3] two to the *muchabhadra*,[4] and two to the *carnacutha* and *harantara* on the other side of the facade. The height of the edifice is divided into twenty-eight parts, of which three are given to the *adhisthana* (base), six to the pillars, three to the entablature, five to the pillars above; two to the entablature, one to the base, two to the neck or *cantha*, four to the cupola, and two to the pinnacle.

The pedestal at the bottom is not included in the height of the temple, but it is equal in height to the base over it.

Under this head may be noticed the designs in Plates XXIII and XXIV, which represent the plan and the front and side elevations of the *vimana* at Sri Rangam, one of the earliest specimens of sacred architecture which the ancients have left us in the south of India. The cupola or dome is crowned with four pinnacles over the front portico, and four more across the former over the principal cell; and in the tabernacle immediately below the cupola, stands the statue of Paravasudeva, a form of Vishnu. The plan of the cell or sanctuary, where the idol of Ranganatha is seen in a recumbent posture, is oval, but that of the front portico square and the outside of the vault is adorned with a sort of tracery-work. The front portico, which extends to a considerable distance from the main cell, is supported by rows of lofty columns; and the whole temple is enclosed by seven square courts, each of them having four pyramidal gateways, one in the middle of each side of the wall. Several of these courts contain private dwelling-houses of Brahmans and other classes. The designs have been taken by an artist on the spot, and the proportions of the different parts of which the temple is composed are, according to his account, as follows: "The whole height of the *vimana* is divided into thirty-two parts,

1. A round ornament at the bottom of the pinnacle.
2. The side niches.
3. The flank ornaments.
4. The front tabernacle.

four are given to the base, three to the pillars, four to the entablature, five to the upper pillars, two to the upper entablature, one to the upper base, two to the *cantha,* four to the cupola, and two to the pinnacle."

A VIMANA CONSISTING OF THREE STOREYS
(See Plates XXVI and XXX)

"The height is twice the breadth, and being divided into forty-eight parts, four are given to the base, eight to the pillar, four to the entablature, seven-and-a-half to the pillar above, three-and-a-half to the entablature, seven to the pillars, three to the entablature, one to the upper base, two to the *cantha,* six to the cupola, and two to the pinnacle."

The first design is made from the foregoing measurement given by Manasara, and the second is taken from the *vimana* of *Vaicuntha Natha*[1] at Canchipuram (Canjeveram). In the lower storey is placed the statue of the god whose name the temple bears; in the upper that of Ranganatha[1] recumbently, and in the third that of Paravasudeva,[1] sitting under the canopy of a cobra de capello. This temple has been selected for a specimen on account of the singularity of the plan, and of the three different deities being worshipped one above another, in as many storeys, of which it is composed.

"The height of this temple is divided into twelve parts, one to the base, two to the pillar, one to the entablature, three-quarters to the pedestal, three-quarters to the base, one-and a-half to the pillar, three-quarters to the entablature, a half to the base, one to the pillar, a half to the entablature, a quarter to the upper base, a half to the *cantha,* one to the cupola, and a half to the pinnacle."

A VIMANA CONSISTING OF FOUR STOREYS
(See Plate XXXI)

> The height of the *vimana* being divided into nineteen parts, one-and-a-half is given to the base, three to the pillar, one-and-a-half to the entablature of the first storey, two and a-half to the pillar, one to the entablature of the second storey, two to the pillar, three-quarters to the entablature of the third storey, one-and-a-half to the pillar, three-quarters to the entablature of the fourth storey, a half to the upper base, one to the *cantha,* two to the cupola, and one to the pinnacle.
>
> The pedestal at the bottom is independent of the rest of the parts, and is equal in height to the base.
>
> The inner pillar of the *carnacutha* (the side niches) of the lower storey, should be placed directly under the outer pillar of the same ornament, in the storey immediately above.

A VIMANA CONSISTING OF FIVE STOREYS
(See Plate XXXII)

> The height is to be divided into twenty-four parts: one-and-a-half to be given to the base, three to the pillar, one-and-a-half to the entablature of the first storey; two-and-a-half to the

1. Vishnu under different forms.

pillar, one-and-a-quarter to the entablature of the second; two-and-a-quarter to the pillar, one to the entablature of the third; two to the pillar, one to the entablature of the fourth; one-and-three-quarters to the pillar, one to the entablature of the fifth; a half to the upper base, one to the *cantha,* two-and-a-half to the cupola, and one-and-a-half to the pinnacle. The pedestal below is equal in height to the base.

Temples of five storeys are found in various parts of southern India; and the design which accompanies, represents one at Rajarayeswaram, in the province of Tanjore.

A VIMANA CONSISTING OF SEVEN STOREYS
(See Plate XXXIII)

The height is divided into thirty-six parts; two to be given to the base, four to the pillar, two to the entablature of the first storey; three-and-a-half to the pillar, one-and-three-quarters to the entablature of the second; three to the pillar, one-and-a-half to the entablature of the third: two-and-a-half to the pillar, one-and-a-half to the entablature of the fourth; two to the pillar, one to the entablature of the fifth; one-and-a-half to the pillar, three-quarters to the entablature of the sixth: one-and-a-quarter to the pillar, five-eighths to the entablature of the seventh; one to the base, one-and-a-half to the *cantha,* two-and-a-half to the cupola, and five-eighths to the pinnacle.

A VIMANA CONSISTING OF TWELVE STOREYS
(See Plate XXXIV)

The whole height is to be divided into eighty-seven parts, four to be given to the base, eight to the pillar, four to the entablature of the first storey; seven to the pillar, three-and-a-half to the entablature of the second; six to the pillar, three to the entablature of the third; five to the pillar, two-and-a-half to the entablature of the fourth; four-and-a-half to the pillar, two-and-a-half to the entablature of the fifth; four to the pillar, two to the entablature of the sixth; three-and-a-half to the pillar, two to the entablature of the seventh; three to the pillar, one-and-a-half to the entablature of the eighth; two-and-a-half to the pillar, one-and-a-quarter to the entablature of the ninth; two and a-half to the pillar, one to the entablature of the tenth; two to the pillar, one to the entablature of the eleventh; one to the upper base, two to the *cantha,* three to the cupola, one-and-a-half to the pinnacle.

A VIMANA CONSISTING OF FIFTEEN STOREYS
(See Plate XXXV)

The height being divided into one hundred and ninety-four parts, seven to be given to the base; thirteen to the pillar, six-and-a-half to the entablature of the first storey; twelve to the pillar, six to the entablature of the second; eleven to the pillar, five-and-a-half to the entablature of the third; ten to the pillar, and five to the entablature of the fourth; nine to the pillar, four-and-a-half to the entablature of the fifth; eight to the pillar, four to the entablature of the sixth, and so on up to the fifteenth storey; the pillars being diminished by half a part regularly, and the entablatures half the height of the pillars over which they are placed; after which one part is given to the upper base, two to the *cantha,* four-and-a-half to the cupola, and one-and-a-quarter to the pinnacle.

The thirty-first chapter of the *Manasara,* as well as the twenty-fourth of the *Mayamata,* treat of *gopuras,* or towers on the gateways of temples; from both which works a few extracts will be given below.

> There are five sorts of gateways, namely, *dwarasobha* (the gate of splendour), *dwarasala* (the gate of the mansion), *dwaraprasada* (the propitious gate), *dwaraharmya* (the gate of the palace), and *dwaragopura* (the turreted gate). The breadth of the principal temple being divided into seven, eight, nine, ten, or eleven parts, six, seven, eight, nine, or ten are to be given to that of the five sorts of *gopuras,* respectively. These five sorts are to be employed in as many courts, by which the temple is to be surrounded.
>
> A *dwarasohha* consists of one or two storeys; a *dwarasala* of from two to four; a *dwaraprasada,* of from three to five; a *dwarahamya,* of from five to seven; and a *dwaragopura,* of from seven to sixteen storeys.
>
> And the breadth of *gopuras,* of the superior sort, may be made twice that of the principal temple, or one and three-quarters, one-and-a-half, or one-and-a-quarter of it: or in *gopuras* of the inferior sort, the breadth of the principal temple being divided into four, five, six, or seven parts, one of these parts should be taken away, and the remainder given to the breadth of the former.
>
> The breadth of the *gopura* at the bottom being divided into three parts; let one of them be given to the void space of the gate in the middle. The height of the door-frame being divided into four parts, let one be given to the pedestal, one to the base, and two to the pillars, around the first storey. Or, the same height being divided into seventeen parts, let five be given to the pedestal, four to the base, and eight to the pillars. The height of the door-frame should be twice its breadth.
>
> The diameter of the *gopura* of a single storey being divided into six parts, three to be given to the interior space, and three to the thickness of the walls.
>
> The diameter of the *gopura* of two storeys being divided into seven parts, four to be given to the interior space, and three to the thickness of the walls.
>
> The diameter of the *gopura* of three storeys being divided into nine parts, four to be given to the interior space, three to the thickness of the walls, and the remainder to the terrace around (*alindra*).
>
> The diameter of the *gopura* of four storeys being divided into ten parts, five to be given to the space inside, four to the thickness of the walls, and one to the terrace around.
>
> The diameter of the *gopura* consisting of seven storeys being divided into thirteen parts, eight to be given to the space inside, three to the thickness of the walls, and two to the terrace around,

and so with the rest.

Various denominations are next given to *gopuras,* such as *sricara, ravi-canta, sawmya, vjjaya, visalaca,* etc., and their characteristic ornaments described with too much minutenesss to be detailed here; and to these succeeds a no less minute enumeration of the various parts which compose *gopuras* of the several heights before-mentioned, of which I shall subjoin the divisions and proportions of those only which consist of one, two, five, six, and twelve storeys, the designs of which accompany this essay.

A DWARASOBHA CONSISTING OF ONE STOREY
(See Plate XXXVI)

The height of the principal pillars of the gate should be three-quarters of the breadth of the pyramid at the bottom, and being divided into four parts, one to be given to the pedestal, one to the base, and two to the pillars, and the whole height of the ornaments over this, is equal to the breadth of the ground-plan; and the same height being divided into four parts, one is to be given to the entablature, one to the *cantha,* two to the cupola, and one to the pinnacles.

A DWARASALA CONSISTING OF TWO STOREYS
(See Plate XXXVII)

The height of the principal pillars of the gate, which should be three-quarters of the breadth of the ground plan, being divided into three and three-quarters parts, three-quarters to be given to the pedestal, one to the base, two to the pillars, and one to the entablature. The height of the pillars in the second storey is one-eighth less than that of the pillars in the first or lower storey, half of which is given to the entablature, half of that to the upper base, twice that to the cavetto above, twice that to the cupola, which should be surmounted by five pinnacles equal in height to half of the cupola.

A GOPURA CONSISTING OF FIVE STOREYS
(See Plates XXXVIII and XXXIX)

The height of the gate-pillars being divided into twenty-one parts, nine to be given to the pedestal, four to the base, and eight to the pillar, and the remainder of the pyramid, from the entablature up to the pinnacle, is in height equal to one-and-a-quarter part of the breadth of the ground plan: and being divided into twenty-three parts, two to be given to the entablature of the first storey; three-and-a-half to the pillar, one-and-three-quarters to the entablature of the second; three to the pillar, one-and-a-half to the entablature of the third; two-and-a-half to the pillar, one-and-a-quarter to the entablature of the fourth: two to the pillar, one to the entablature of the fifth; one to the cavetto, two-and-a-half to the dome, and one to the pinnacle.

A GOPURA CONSISTING OF SIX STOREYS
(See Plate XL)

The height of the gate-pillars, which is three-quarters of the breadth of the ground plan, being divided into four-and-a-half parts, one-and-a-half to be given to the pedestal, one to the base, and two to the pillars; and the upper part of the pyramid, which is equal in height to the breadth of the ground plan, being divided into twenty-nine parts, two are to be given to the entablature of the first storey; four to the pillar, one-and-three-quarters to the entablature of the second; three-and-a-half to the pillar, one-and-three-quarters to the entablature of the third; three to the pillar, one-and-a-half to the entablature of the fourth; two-and-a-half to the pillar, one-and-a-half to the entablature of the fifth; two to the pillar, one to the entablature of the sixth; one to the cavetto, two-and-a-half to the dome, and one-and-a-half to the pinnacle.

A GOPURA CONSISTING OF TWELVE STOREYS
(See Plates XLI and XLII)

The height of the gate-pillars is three-quarters of the breadth of the plan, and it being divided into five parts, two to be given to the pedestal, one to the base, and two to the pillar. The upper part is equal in height to twice the breadth of the ground plan; and the same being divided into eighty-five parts, three-and-a-half to be given to the entablature of the first storey; seven to the pillar, three-and-a-half to the entablature of the second; six and a-half to the pillar, three-and-a-half to the entablature of the third; six to the pillar, three to the entablature of the fourth; five-and-a-half to the pillar, two-and-three-quarters to the entablature of the fifth; five to the pillar, two-and-a-half to the entablature of the sixth; four-and-a-half to the pillar, two-and-a-half to the entablature of the seventh; four to the pillar, two to the entablature of the eighth; three-and-a-half to the pillar, one-and-three-quarters to the entablature of the ninth; three to the pillar, one-and-a-half to the entablature of the tenth; two-and-a-half to the pillar, one-and-a-quarter to the entablature of the eleventh; two to the pillar, one to the entablature of the twelfth; one to the upper pedestal, one and three quarters to the cavetto, three-and-a-half to the dome, and one-and-a-half to the pinnacles.

Having given the proportions of the different parts of pyramidal temples and gateways, we may be permitted to indulge in a few words relative to their general appearance, and to the ideas which this is calculated to impress on the mind.

An eminent author makes the architectural sublime to consist "in magnitude, height of the buildings, and solidity of the materials;" another author, "in splendour, magnificence, and an imposing appearance." These characteristics of the sublime, most of the Indian temples possess in an eminent degree, independently of that sort of light betwixt gloom and glare, which increases the sublimity in architecture; and in beholding these majestic and stupendous works, we are struck with admiration and respect, and animated with emotions of piety, virtue, and religion.

If we enter into the minutiae of the art, which solely depend on scientific proportion, and on the skilful application of mechanic powers, we are led to wonder at the success of the artist in his attempts at the sublime, and to express our astonishment at the physical powers employed in the superstructure.

Of all the modes of building invented by man, the pyramid seems to be best calculated to produce these impressions. It must be acknowledged, however, that the pyramidal buildings of India are of much less dimensions than those of Egypt, and that the former have too great a profusion of ornaments. If we examine the exterior of these temples, we should discover with what skill the bulk of the edifice is shown to advantage, and how admirably the parts are formed for the eye to embrace the whole, at the same time that the sight is bewildered with the infinite variety of decorations. The interior, also, is so constructed as to cast over it a visible oblivion, that indispensable requisite of the sublime.

I shall now close this essay, with the following short account of the mode of preparing *chunam*, or cement, as practised by the artists in India.

Chunam is prepared in the interior of India from a gravelly sort of lime-stone dug out of quarries, and along the coast from shells washed out of salt-water marshes. Of the two, the shell *chunam* is generally considered the strongest and most durable. The following is the mode of preparing stone *chunam*: The pebbles or gravel stones are first beat with wooden pestles, to separate the alluminous clay which adheres to them; after they are thus cleaned, they are sorted, as of a white or brown quality. In some places, the stone is burnt by simply laying alternate layers of stone and charcoal on the ground, in the proportion of two parts of charcoal to one of stone, and thus allowed to burn out. The stone, after being burnt, is slacked by laying small quantities in heaps and throwing water on them; and as soon as the heat begins, the whole is mixed up together and stirred about till it is reduced to a dry powder. The lime is now considered fit for the use of the builder. Shell *chunam* is manufactured much in the same way, excepting that it is again cleansed by the manufacturer in a dry state, by strewing it down against the wind, after the manner that corn is winnowed to separate the chaff. The burning, also, is differently performed: the charcoal is mixed up with the shells, and burnt in large open kilns, with a grated bottom and longitudinal flue, communicating with four or more lateral openings. The stone *chunam* forms a coarse sandy powder, and the shell a very fine impalpable one. From these two substances all the mortar for building throughout India is prepared; they are mixed with clean sharp river sand in various proportions, according to the use for which they are intended. For brick work, from one part and a-half to three of sand is mixed, with one or two of the fine slacked lime; for the coarse undercoat plastering, from one to two of sand with two of lime; and for the last and fine upper coating, two to three of sand with one of lime. When the mortar is prepared for the brick work in rough plastering, it is simply beat up with pure water in long stone troughs, with wooden pestles about a yard-and-a-half long and shod with iron hoops. *Chunam* intended for fine plastering and ornamental works is ground by women, on an oblong granite stone and a cylindrical upper stone about four inches in diameter; the mixture is sometimes ground two, three, and four times, to bring it to the required fineness and purity. In all the operations of *chunam* work, *jaggery* water, i.e. a solution of molasses or coarse sugar, is invariably added by the builders, and its use appears to have prevailed from the remotest ages. There are various opinions among the modern practitioners regarding its usefulness, but those who have had the most extensive practice in building, hold it as an indispensable ingredient in the formation of a durable and hard cement; and it is stated that the operator evidently perceives the dissolvent property of the *jaggery* water, on its being tempered with the prepared mortar. It is supposed that it tends very much to the intimate union of the coarse particles of the lime with the sharp sand, on account of the saccharine acid in the molasses, and the gaseous principle of its earthy parts, causing a quicker chemical induration of the mortar than would be effected by mere application of pure water conjoined with the absorption of the hardening substance of the atmospheric air.

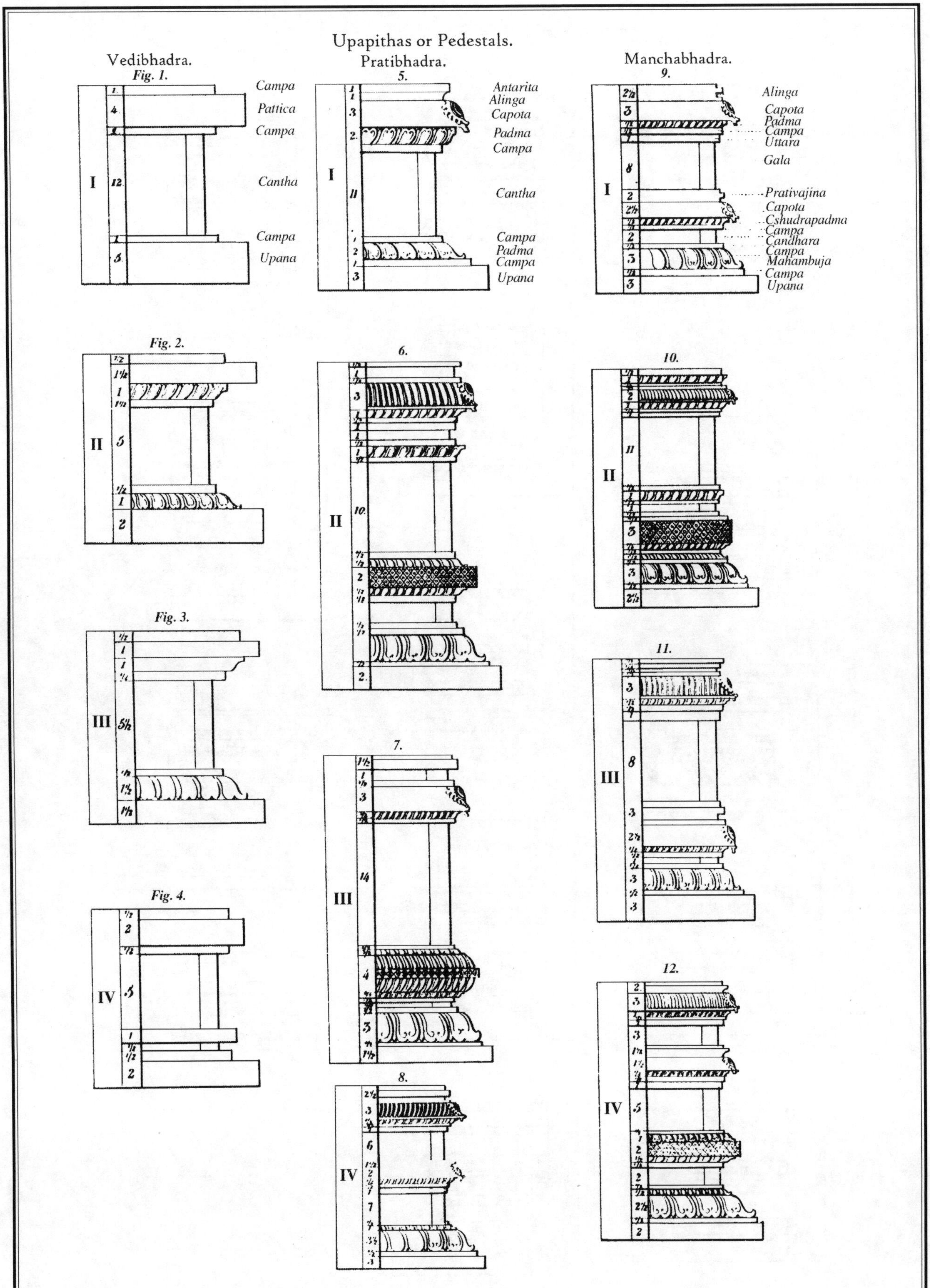
Upapithas or Pedestals.
Vedibhadra.
Pratibhadra.
Manchabhadra.
Fig. 1.
5.
9.
Campa
Pattica
Campa
Cantha
Campa
Upana
Antarita
Alinga
Capota
Padma
Campa
Cantha
Campa
Padma
Campa
Upana
Alinga
Capota
Padma
Campa
Uttara
Gala
Prativajina
Capota
Cshudrapadma
Campa
Candhara
Campa
Mahambuja
Campa
Upana
Fig. 2.
6.
10.
Fig. 3.
11.
7.
Fig. 4.
12.
8.
I
II
III
IV

Pl. II

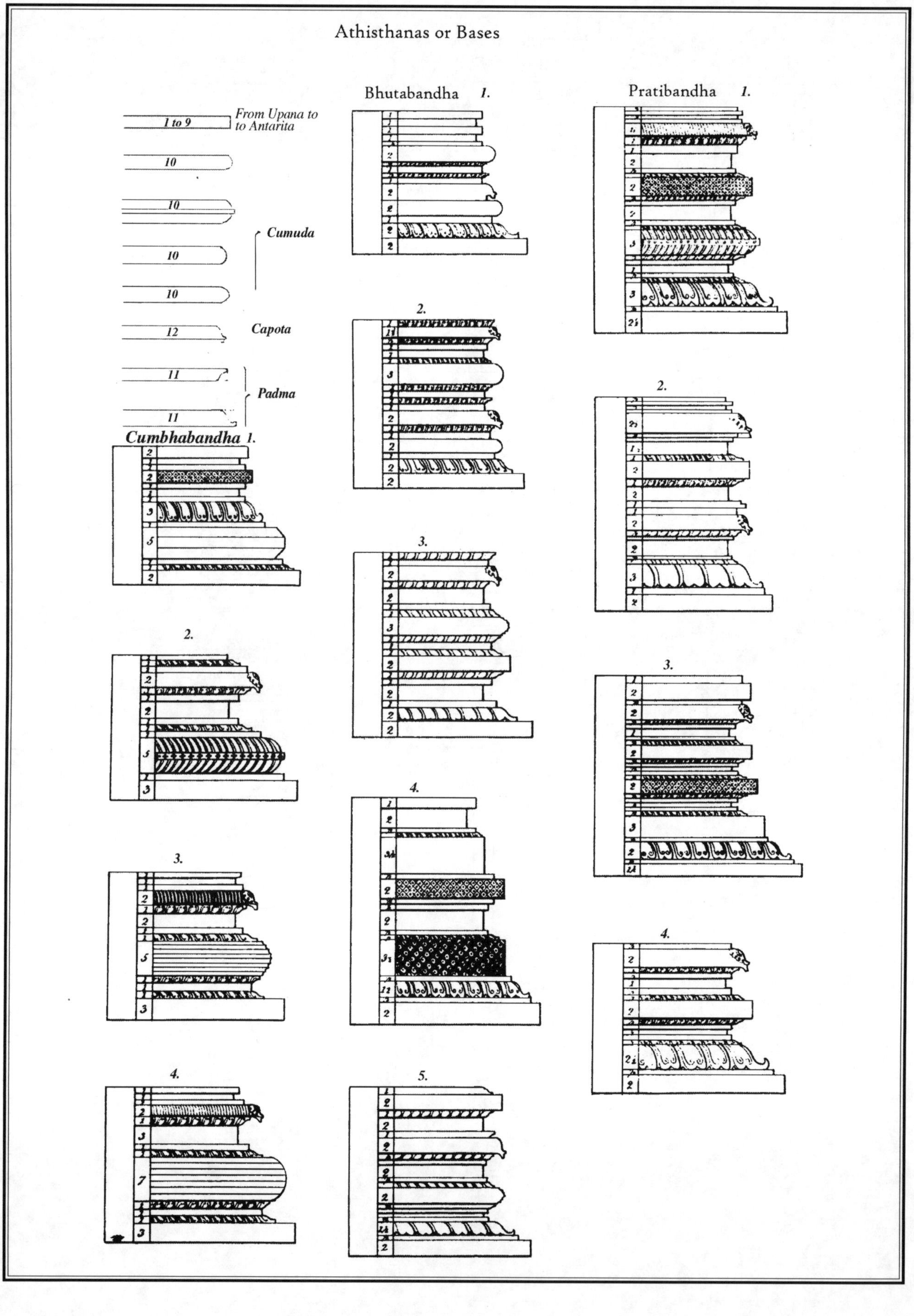

Athisthanas or Bases
1 to 9
From Upana to to Antarita
10
Cumuda
Capota
12
11
Padma
Cumbhabandha 1.
2.
3.
4.
Bhutabandha 1.
2.
3.
4.
5.
Pratibandha 1.
2.
3.
4.

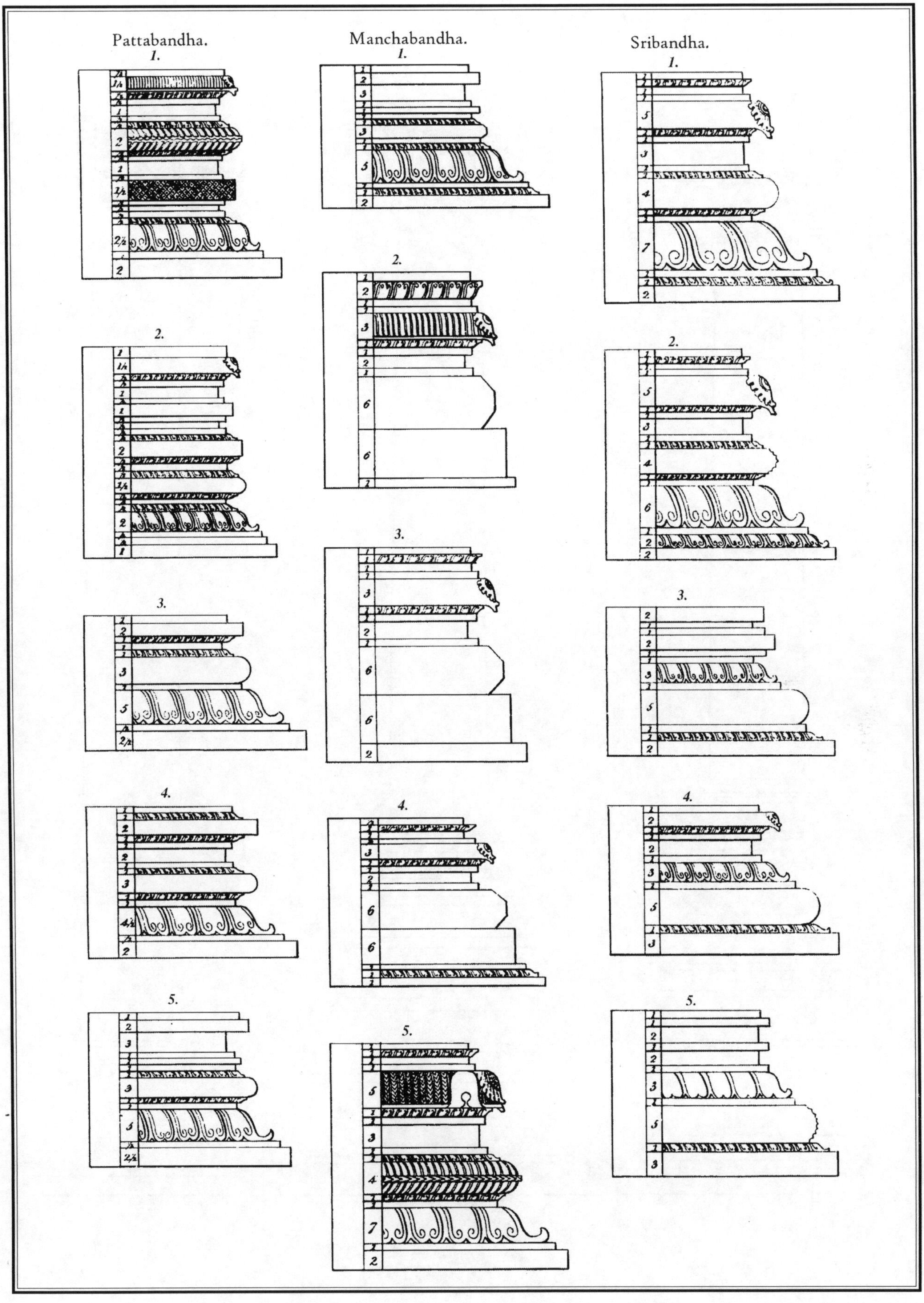
Pattabandha.
1.
2.
3.
4.
5.
Manchabandha.
1.
2.
3.
4.
5.
Sribandha.
1.
2.
3.
4.
5.

Pl. IV

Pl. VI

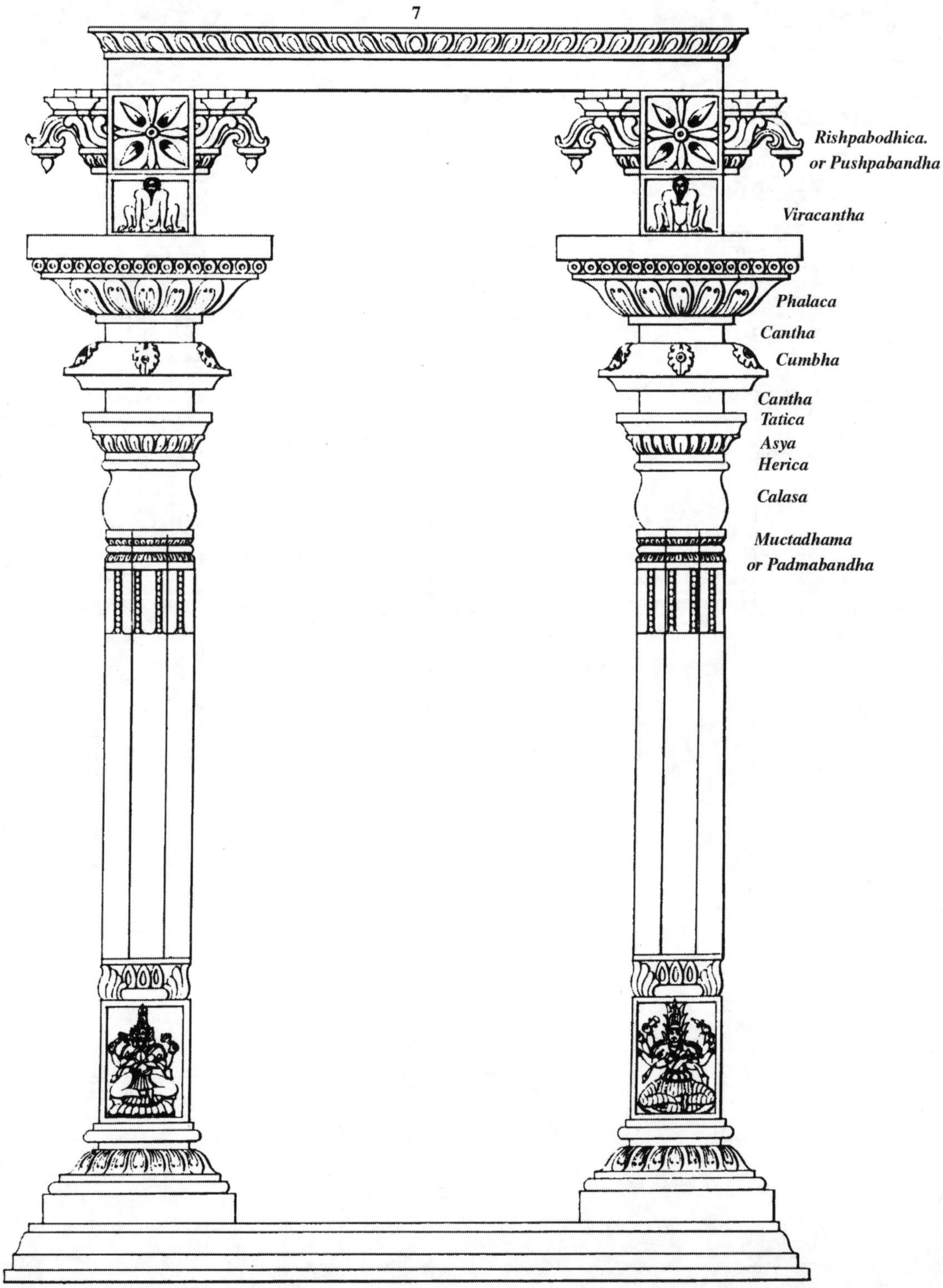
7
Rishpabodhica.
or Pushpabandha
Viracantha
Phalaca
Cantha
Cumbha
Cantha
Tatica
Asya
Herica
Calasa
Muctadhama
or Padmabandha

8

9

10

Pl. X

11

12

Pl. XII

13

14

Pl. XIV

15

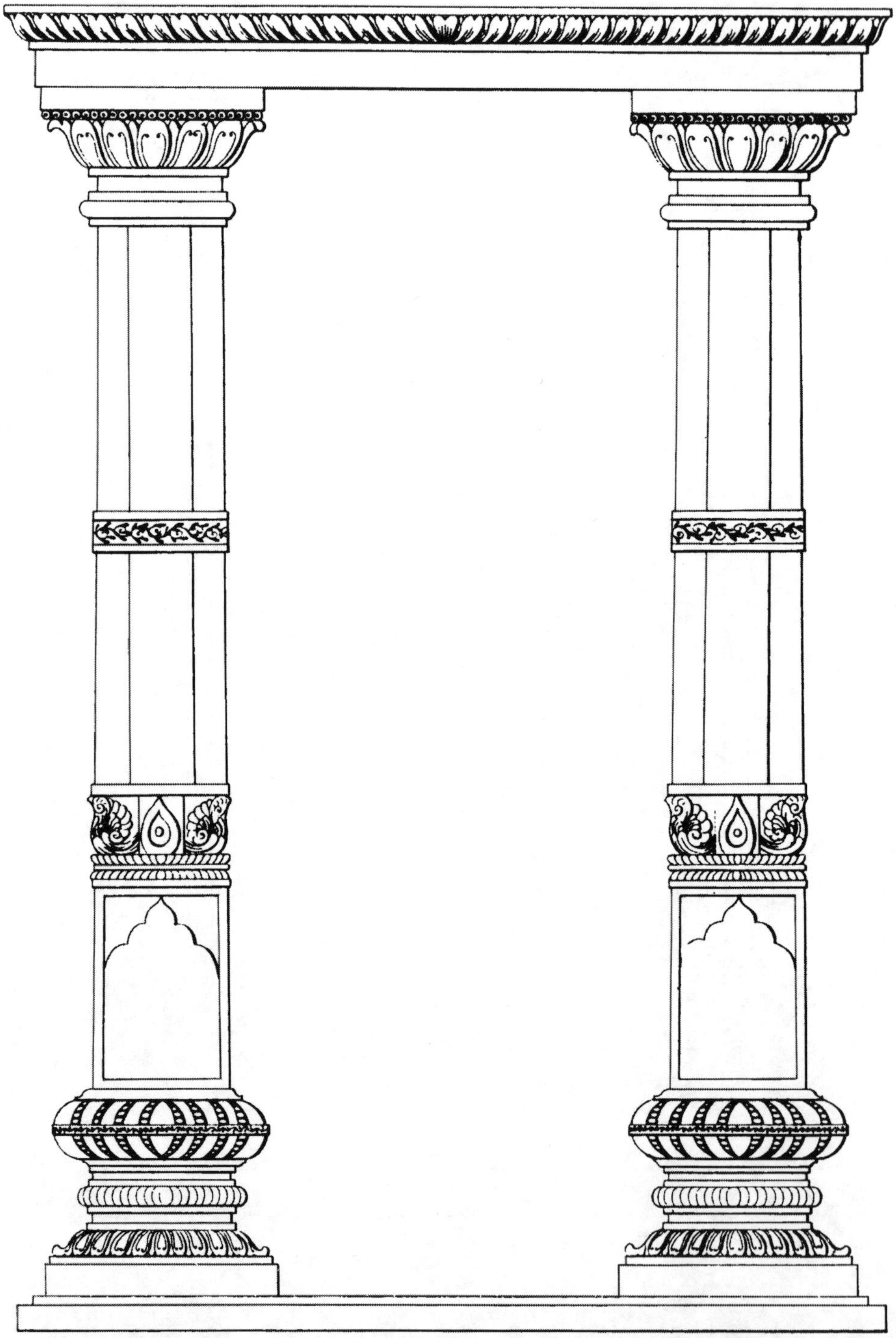

Pl. XV

Pl. XVI

19

20

Prastaras or Entablatures

1

2

3

4

Pl. XX

A Vimana consisting of a single storey.

A Vimana consisting of two storeys.

The Vimana of Sri Rangam. Front Elevation

The Vimana at Sri Rangam.

Side Elevation

Another Vimana of two storeys.

A Vimana consisting of three storeys.

Another Vimana consisting of three storeys.

A Vimana of two storeys.

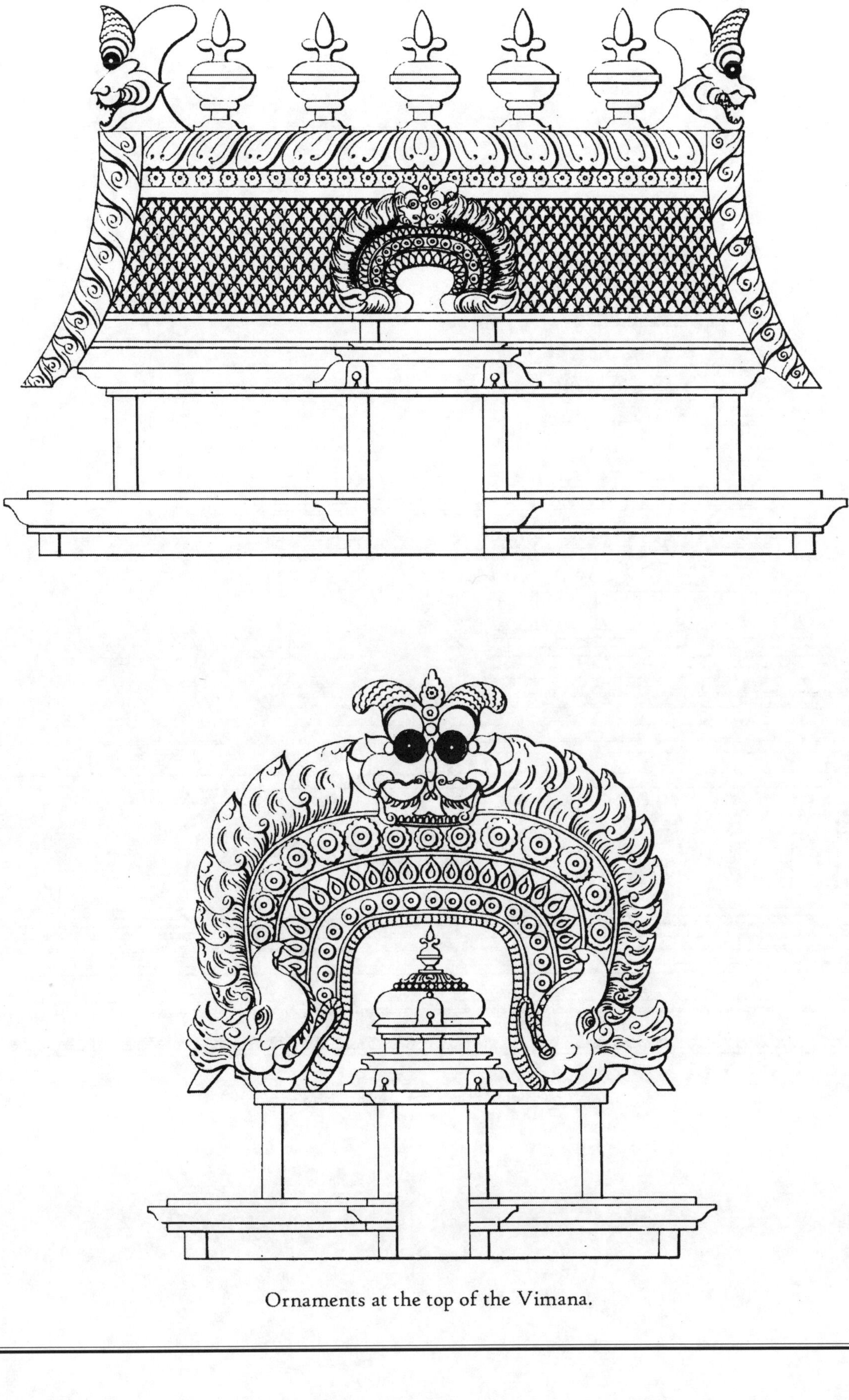

Ornaments at the top of the Vimana.

The Vimana of Vaycunthanatha at Canjeveram.

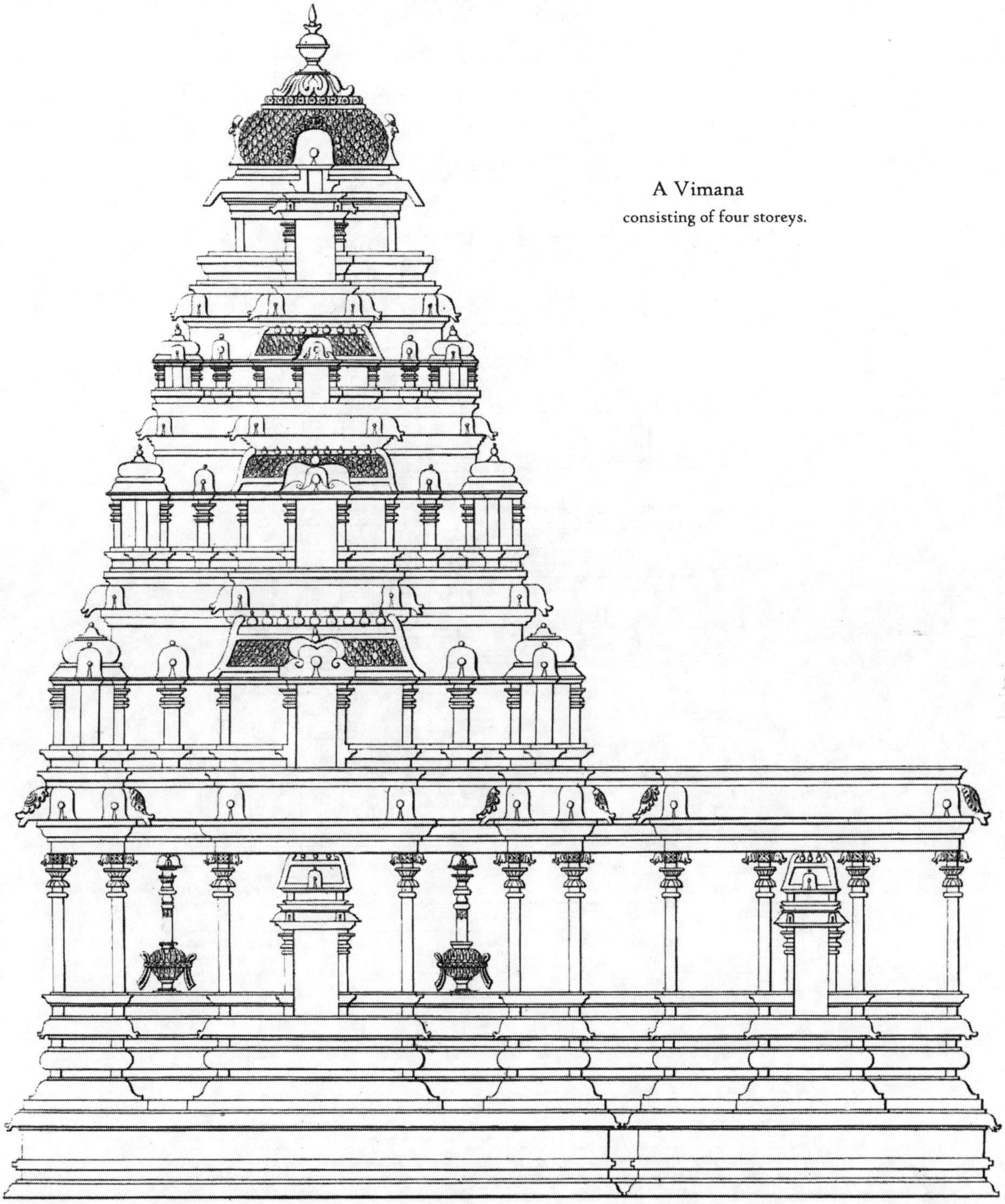

A Vimana
consisting of four storeys.

A Vimana consisting of five storeys.

A Vimana consisting of seven storeys.

Pl. XXXIV

A Vimana consisting of twelve storeys.

A Vimana consisting of fifteen storeys.

A Gopura consisting of one storey.

A Gopura consisting of two storeys.

A Gopura consisting of five storeys.

A Gopura consisting of five storeys.
Side Elevation.

Pl. XL

A Gopura consisting of six storeys.

Pl. XLI

A Gopura consisting of twelve storeys.

Pl. XLII

A Gopura consisting of twelve storeys.

Plan of Villages &c.

Dandaca.

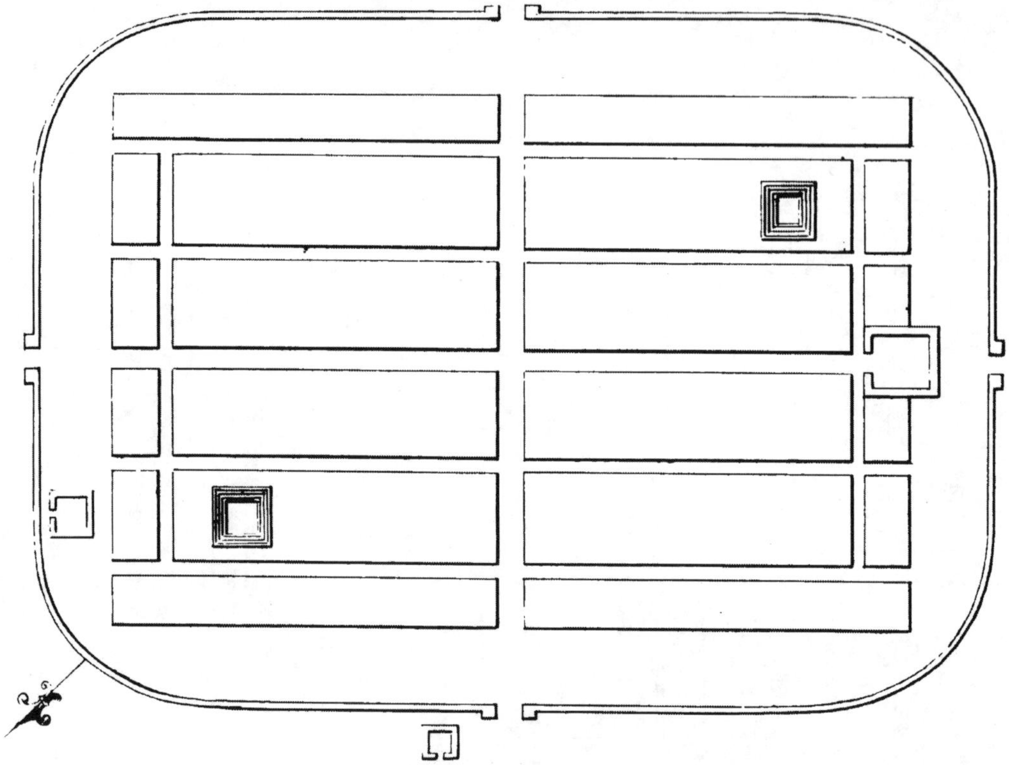

Sarvatobhadra

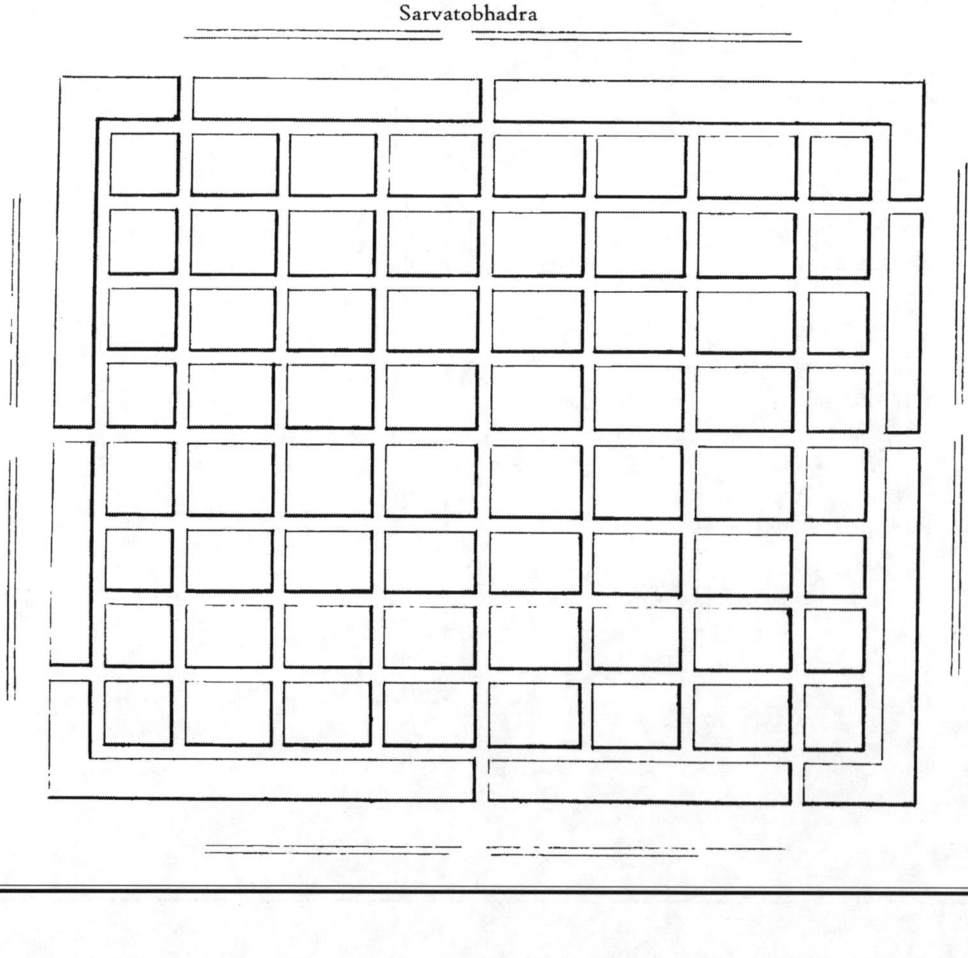

Nandyavartta.

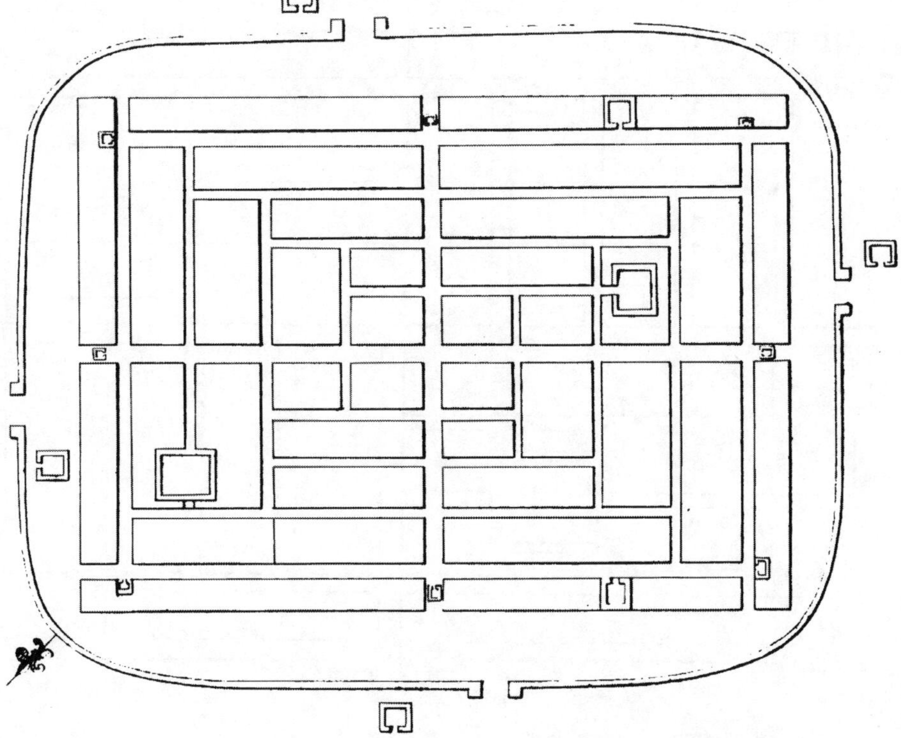

Padmaca.

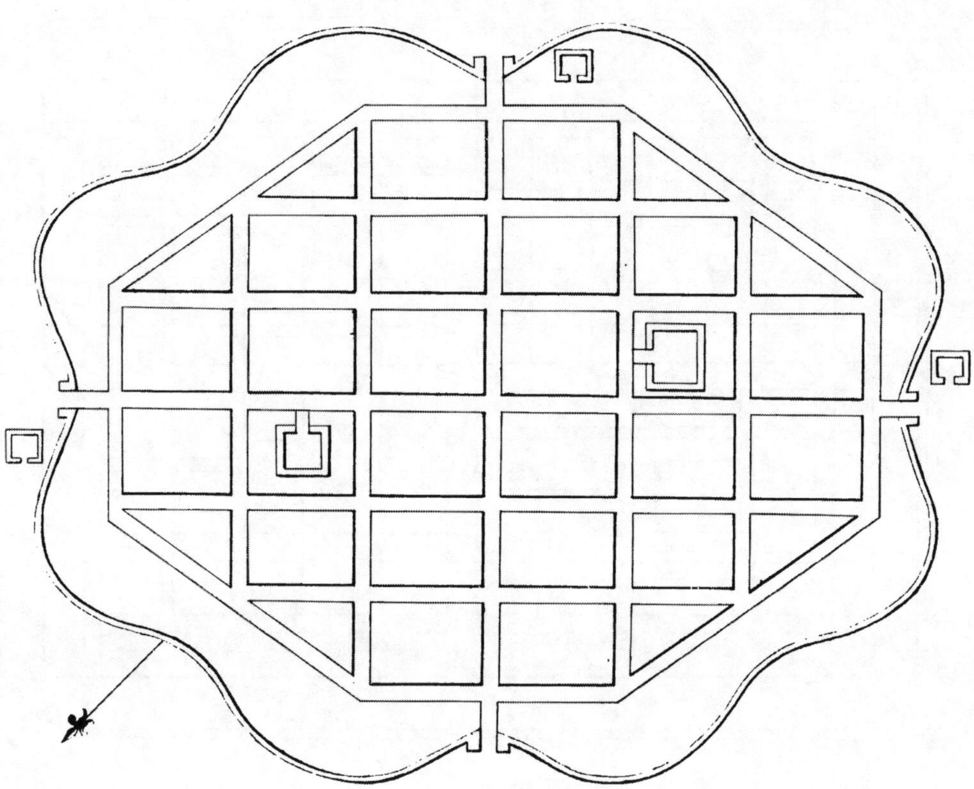

Swastica.

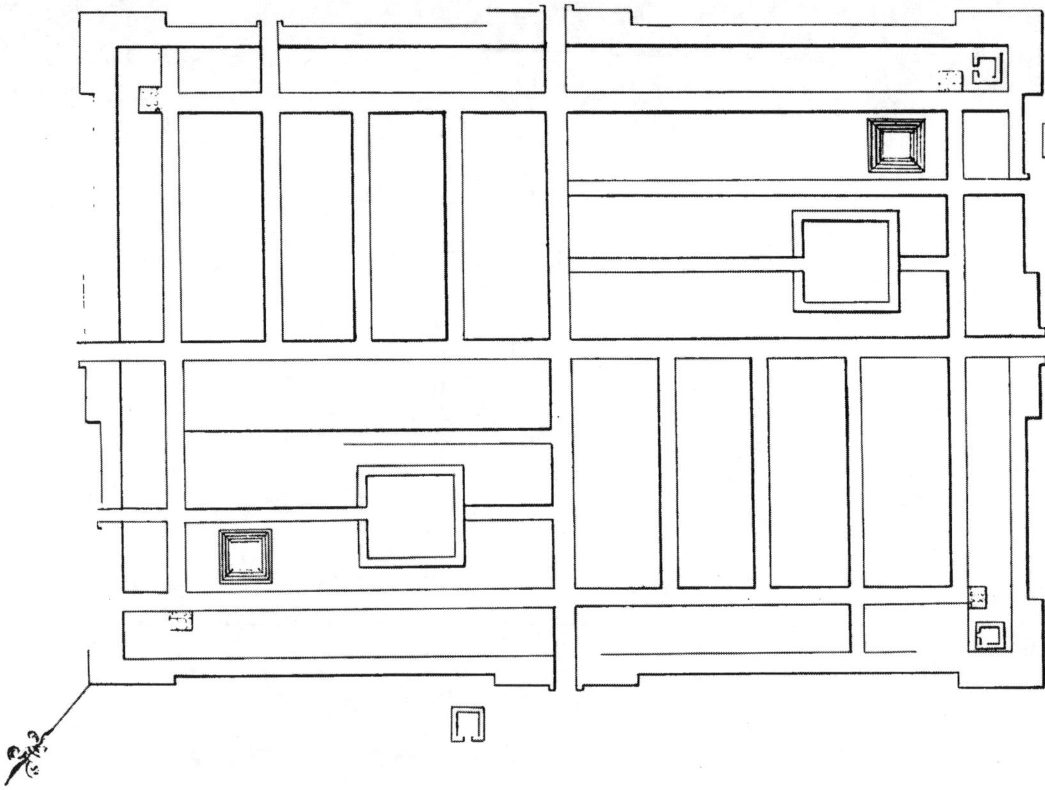

Prastara.

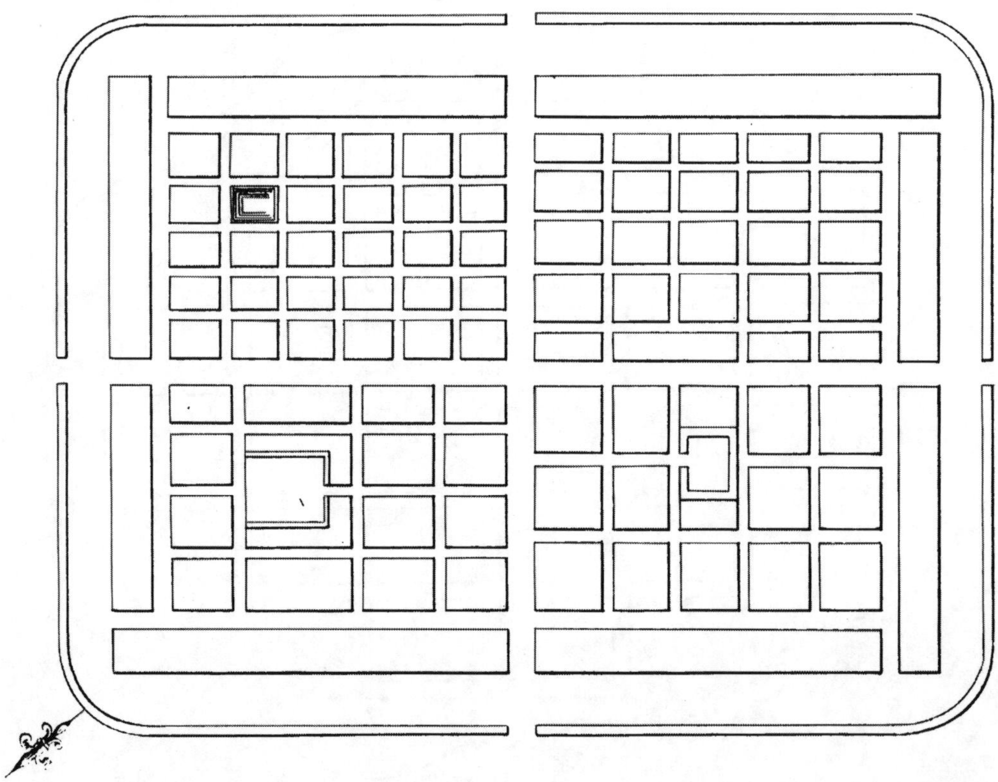

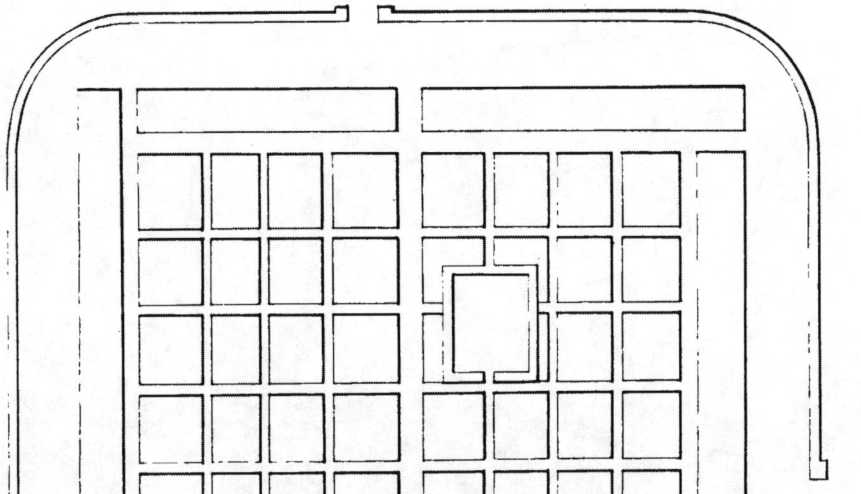

Pl. XLVII

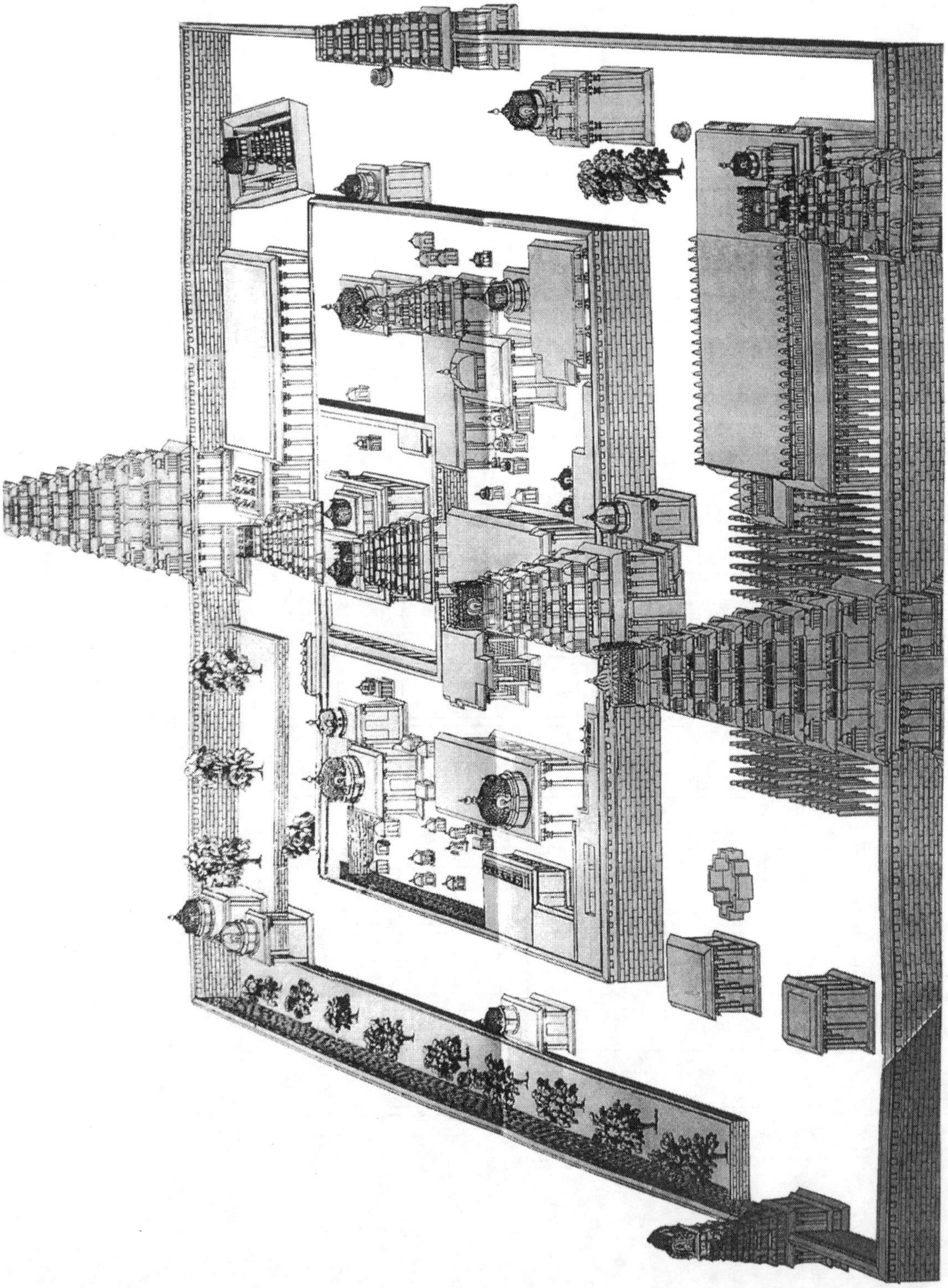

The Pagoda of Tiruvalur.

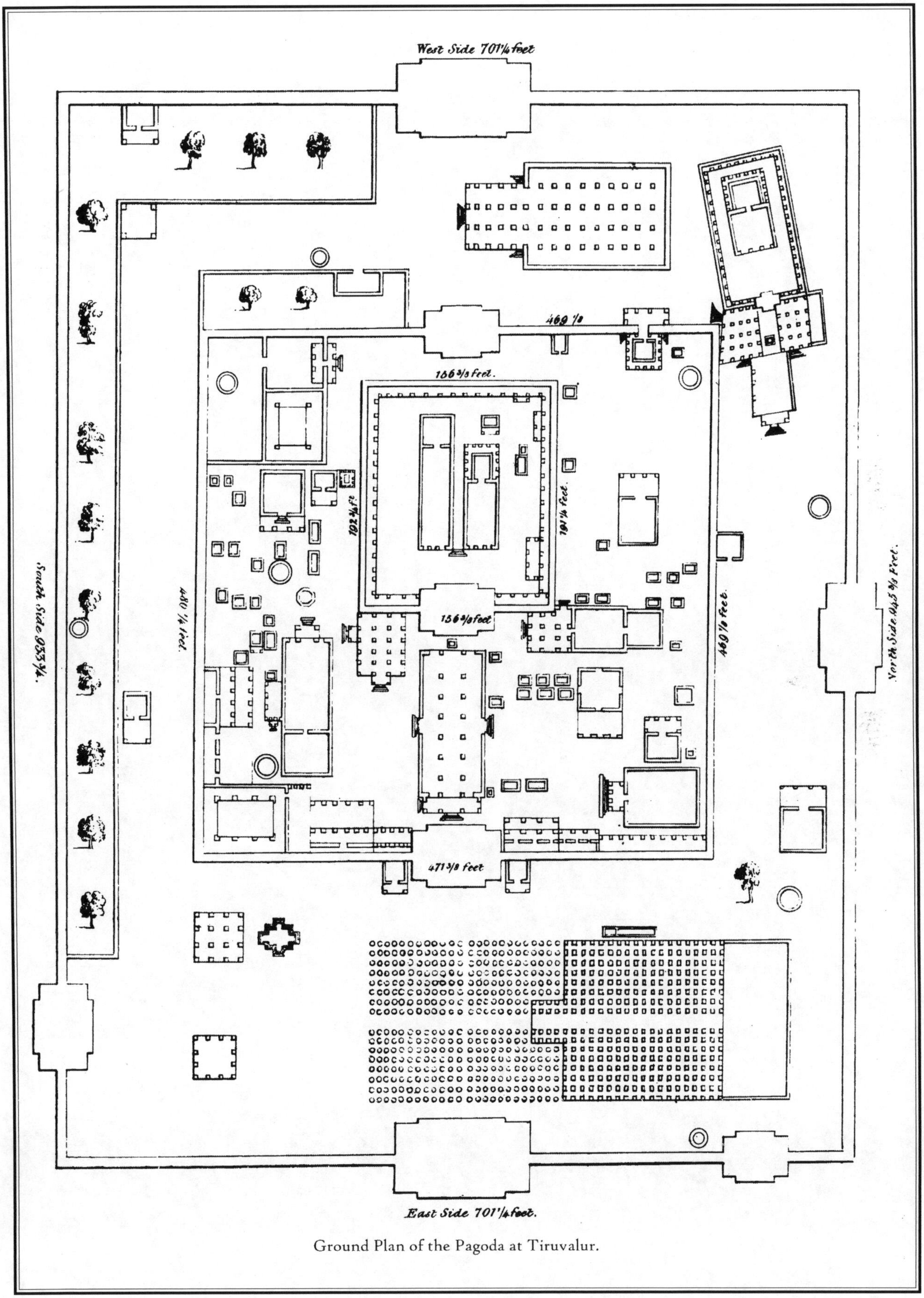

Ground Plan of the Pagoda at Tiruvalur.